A-Z

YORK
COLLEGE

Workbook

A-Z
CHEMISTRY
Workbook

Andrew Hunt

Hodder & Stoughton
A MEMBER OF THE HODDER HEADLINE GROUP

Orders: please contact Bookpoint Ltd, 130 Milton Park, Abingdon,
Oxon OX14 4SB. Telephone: (44) 01235 827720, Fax: (44) 01235 400454.
Lines are open from 9.00–6.00, Monday to Saturday, with a 24 hour message
answering service. Email address: orders@bookpoint.co.uk

British Library Cataloguing in Publication Data
A catalogue record for this title is available from The British Library

ISBN 0 340 79982X

First published 2001
Impression number   10 9 8 7 6 5 4 3 2 1
Year   2005 2004 2003 2002 2001

Copyright © 2001 Andrew Hunt

Typeset by Florence Production Ltd, Stoodleigh, Devon
Printed in Great Britain for Hodder & Stoughton Educational,
a division of Hodder Headline Plc, 338 Euston Road, London NW1 3BH
by Martins The Printers Ltd, Berwick Upon Tweed

Contents

Acknowledgements

I am particularly grateful to Robin Hillman who read the whole workbook with great care and checked the answers. His advice has helped to make this Workbook more accurate and more helpful to students. My thanks too to the series editor Ian Marcousé and the team at Hodder & Stoughton including Tim Gregson-Williams, Alexia Chan and Diana Bateman.

Introduction

This workbook will help you learn and revise Chemistry. During your course, this workbook will be ideal for checking that you understand the concepts you have just been taught. The A–Z format makes this exceptionally easy to do. If you work through the exercises, questions and puzzles in this book, you will study all the key ideas in AS and A2 Chemistry courses.

The labels AS and A2, added to the topic titles, help you to spot the topics relevant at each stage of your course. There are just a few topics which appear in the AS modules of some courses, but the A2 modules of others, so these are labelled AS/A2. Other topics appear twice, with easier exercises at AS level but more challenging problems for A2. Bear in mind that, towards the end of an A2 course, you are expected to gain an overview of the chemical ideas as a whole, so at that stage all topics in the workbook are relevant to your studies.

This workbook can make your learning and revision more efficient by fitting the work into moments of your days when you might otherwise do nothing. The emphasis throughout is on thinking rather than on writing. The activities are all short so you can complete some worthwhile learning when travelling to school or college, during some spare minutes during a lunch break or while waiting for a class to begin.

All you need is a pen or pencil. For a few of the problems you will find it helpful to have a calculator. Refer to the Periodic table on page viii for the atomic numbers and relative atomic masses of the elements. All other data is provided as you need it.

If you take some care with your responses, you will build up a set of notes that you can use for revision later. Consider using a variety of colours to make the text and images you create on the page more memorable.

You will find answers to all the exercises, questions and puzzles on pages 146–164. If you would like explanations for the answers, turn to the related key-term entries in the Complete A–Z Chemistry Handbook.

Towards the end of a full A-level course you will find it helpful to check your knowledge and understanding with the three multiple choice tests on pages 124–145. Each test covers a wide range of topics and will help you prepare for a synoptic examination.

Andrew Hunt

Periodic table

Group

	1	2											3	4	5	6	7	8
Period 1	1 **H** Hydrogen 1																	2 **He** Helium 4

Key:

Atomic number
Symbol
Name
Relative atomic mass

Transition elements

Period	1	2											3	4	5	6	7	8
2	3 **Li** Lithium 7	4 **Be** Beryllium 9											5 **B** Boron 11	6 **C** Carbon 12	7 **N** Nitrogen 14	8 **O** Oxygen 16	9 **F** Fluorine 19	10 **Ne** Neon 20
3	11 **Na** Sodium 23	12 **Mg** Magnesium 24											13 **Al** Aluminium 27	14 **Si** Silicon 28	15 **P** Phosphorus 31	16 **S** Sulfur 32	17 **Cl** Chlorine 35.5	18 **Ar** Argon 40
4	19 **K** Potassium 39	20 **Ca** Calcium 40	21 **Sc** Scandium 45	22 **Ti** Titanium 48	23 **V** Vanadium 51	24 **Cr** Chromium 52	25 **Mn** Manganese 55	26 **Fe** Iron 56	27 **Co** Cobalt 59	28 **Ni** Nickel 59	29 **Cu** Copper 63.5	30 **Zn** Zinc 65.4	31 **Ga** Gallium 70	32 **Ge** Germanium 73	33 **As** Arsenic 75	34 **Se** Selenium 79	35 **Br** Bromine 80	36 **Kr** Krypton 84
5	37 **Rb** Rubidium 85	38 **Sr** Strontium 88	39 **Y** Yttrium 89	40 **Zr** Zirconium 91	41 **Nb** Niobium 93	42 **Mo** Molybdenum 96	43 **Tc** Technetium 99	44 **Ru** Ruthenium 101	45 **Rh** Rhodium 103	46 **Pd** Palladium 106	47 **Ag** Silver 108	48 **Cd** Cadmium 112	49 **In** Indium 115	50 **Sn** Tin 119	51 **Sb** Antimony 122	52 **Te** Tellurium 128	53 **I** Iodine 127	54 **Xe** Xenon 131
6	55 **Cs** Caesium 133	56 **Ba** Barium 137	57 ▶ **La** Lanthanum 139	72 **Hf** Hafnium 178	73 **Ta** Tantalum 181	74 **W** Tungsten 184	75 **Re** Rhenium 186	76 **Os** Osmium 190	77 **Ir** Iridium 192	78 **Pt** Platinum 195	79 **Au** Gold 197	80 **Hg** Mercury 201	81 **Ti** Thallium 204	82 **Pb** Lead 207	83 **Bi** Bismuth 209	84 **Po** Polonium	85 **At** Astatine	86 **Rn** Radon
7	87 **Fr** Francium	88 **Ra** Radium 226	89 ▶▶ **Ac** Actinium	104 **Rf** Rutherfordium	105 **Db** Dubnium	106 **Sg** Seaborgram	107 **Bh** Bohrium	108 **Hs** Hassium	109 **Mt** Meitnerium	110 **Uun** Ununnilium	111 **Uuu** Unununium	112 **Uub** Unununium						

▶ Lanthanoid elements

58 **Ce** Cerium 140	59 **Pr** Praseodymium 141	60 **Nd** Neodymium 144	61 **Pm** Promethium	62 **Sm** Samarium 150	63 **Eu** Europium 152	64 **Gd** Gadolinium 157	65 **Tb** Terbium 159	66 **Dy** Dysprosium 163	67 **Ho** Holmium 165	68 **Er** Erbium 167	69 **Tm** Thulium 169	70 **Yb** Ytterbium 173	71 **Lu** Lutetium 175

▶▶ Actinoid elements

90 **Th** Thorium 232	91 **Pa** Protactinium 231	92 **U** Uranium 238	93 **Np** Neptunium 237	94 **Pu** Plutonium 239	95 **Am** Americium	96 **Cm** Curium	97 **Bk** Berkelium	98 **Cf** Californium	99 **Es** Einsteinium	100 **Fm** Fermium	101 **Md** Mendelevium	102 **No** Nobelium	103 **Lr** Lawrencium

Note: Relative atomic masses are shown only for elements which have stable isotopes or isotopes with a very long half-life.

A–Z Questions

Complete this worked example with the help of data from the Periodic table on page viii.

Example: A 41 g sample of phosphonic acid, H_3PO_3, was dissolved in water and the volume of the solution was made up to 1 dm^3. 20.0 cm^3 of this solution was required to react with 25.0 cm^3 of a 0.80 mol dm^{-1} solution of sodium hydroxide. What is the equation for the reaction?

ANSWER

The molar mass of phosponic acid = ... g mol^{-1}

Amount of acid in 1 dm^3 of solution = $\dfrac{41\ g}{............\ g\ mol^{-1}}$ = ... mol

The concentration of the acid = ... mol dm^{-3}

The amount of acid used to neutralise the alkali = 0.020 dm^3 × .... mol dm^{-3}

$\qquad\qquad\qquad\qquad\qquad\qquad$ = ... mol

The amount of NaOH neutralised = ... dm^3 × 0.080 mol dm^{-3}

$\qquad\qquad\qquad\qquad\qquad$ = ... mol

The ratio of the amounts: .... mol H_3PO_3: .... mol NaOH

The equation is

$\qquad$ $H_3PO_3(aq)$ + ...NaOH(aq) → .... (aq) + ...H_2O(l)

Now answer this question.

A solution of a metal carbonate, M_2CO_3, was prepared by dissolving 7.46 g of the anhydrous solid in water to give one litre of solution. 25.0 cm^3 of the carbonate solution reacted with 27.0 cm^3 of a 0.1 mol dm^{-3} solution of hydrochloric acid. Calculate the molar mass of M_2CO_3 and hence the molar mass of the element M.

Molar mass of M_2CO_3 = ...

Molar mass of M $\qquad$ = ...

1

Acids^{AS}

Complete these statements about the characteristic reactions of acids by filling in the missing formulae or numbers.

Acids:

- form solutions in water with a pH below .... ;

- change the colours of acid–base .... ;

- in aqueous solution react with metals such as zinc to produce hydrogen gas

  $Mg(s) +$ .... $HCl(aq) \rightarrow$ .... $(aq) + H_2(g)$

- in aqueous solution react with .... for example ....
  to form carbon dioxide gas and water;

  ....(s) $+ 2HCl(aq) \rightarrow CaCl_2(aq) + CO_2(g) + H_2O(l)$

- in aqueous solution react with .... oxides to form salts and water.

  $MgO(s) + H_2SO_4(aq) \rightarrow$ ....(aq) $+$ ....(l)

What do all solutions of acids in water have in common?

....

Write the names and formulae of these acids into the appropriate column in the table: chloric(1) acid, ethanoic acid, hydrochloric acid, nitric acid, sulfuric acid, sulfurous acid.

Strong acid	Weak acid

Activation energy^AS

Which of the numbered statements are true and which are false for this diagram?

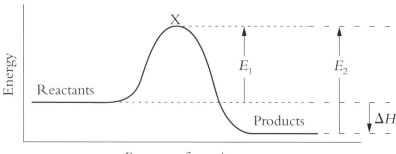

Progress of reaction

1   E_1 is the activation energy for the forward reaction. ....

2   E_2 is the activation energy for the reverse reaction. ....

3   ΔH is the sum of the standard enthalpy changes of formation for the products.
....

4   The forward reaction is endothermic. ....

5   The reverse reaction is exothermic. ....

6   X represents the activated complex. ....

7   A catalyst for the reaction gives a reaction pathway with lower values for
E_1 and E_2. ....

Now fill in the blanks in these sentences.

Activation energies account for the way in which reaction rates vary with ....
At a higher .... there are are more molecules with enough energy to react
when they ....

The .... energies for many reactions in biochemical systems are around
50 kJ mol^{-1} and the rate for these reactions the rate of reaction .... for each
10 K rise in temperature.

Acyl chlorides[A2]

Complete this diagram to summarise the reactions of ethanoyl chloride to show how it acylates ethanol, ammonia and ethylamine. When complete, the diagram should show both the structural formulae and the name of each of the organic compounds.

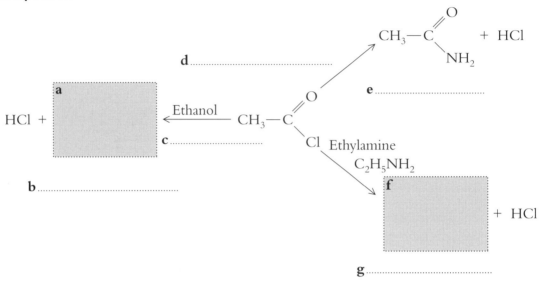

All these reactions are .... at room temperature.

Addition–elimination reactions[A2]

With a coloured pen, draw in the curly arrows missing from this description of the mechanism for the reaction of ethanol with ethanoyl chloride. Name the organic product. Also write one of these terms against each of the three reaction arrows: addition, elimination, gain and loss of protons.

Addition polymers^{AS/A2}

Fill in the missing names and structures.

Monomer (name and structure)	Polymer (name and structure)
a H—C=C—H with H, H (ethene structure)	**b**
c Propene	**d** Poly(propene) or polypropylene $\left[\begin{array}{cc} H & H \\ -C-C- \\ H & CH_3 \end{array} \right]_n$
H—C=C—H with H, phenyl ring Phenylethene	**d**
e Chloroethene	**f** Poly(chloroethene) or polyvinylchloride (PVC)
g F—C=C—F with F, F (tetrafluoroethene structure)	**h**

Addition reactions[AS]

Complete the statements and then the equation for the example.

An addition reaction is a reaction in which .... molecules add together to form a .... product.

Addition reactions are characteristic of .... compounds such as the .... Bromine, for example, adds to ethene to form the addition product ....

Air pollution[AS]

Identify each type of air pollution described in the table.

Description	Type of pollution
A type of pollution produced when burning fuels or an industrial process release oxides into the air. Sulfur dioxide, SO_2, and nitrogen oxides, NO_x, form when fossil fuels burn. These primary pollutants are converted to secondary pollutants by chemical reactions in the air.	
Some gases in the air keep the surface of the Earth about 30 °C warmer that it would be if there were no atmosphere. Combustion of fossil fuels is enhancing this effect, leading to a rise in mean temperatures worldwide.	
Pollution caused by gases from motor vehicles on still, sunny days. The primary pollutants are nitrogen oxides and unburnt hydrocarbons. Bright sunlight during the middle of the day sets off chemical reactions involving oxygen in the air. The products are the secondary pollutants.	
CFCs escape into the atmosphere where they are so stable that they last for many years, long enough for them to diffuse up to the stratosphere. In the stratosphere the intense ultraviolet light from the Sun splits CFCs into free radicals including chlorine atoms.	

Alcohols^{AS}

Answer questions 1–12 by writing a letter for the appropriate structures in the spaces provided. You can use a structure more than once.

1 2-methylpropan-2-ol: ....

2 A secondary alcohol: ....

3 A functional group isomer of C: ....

4 Formed by heating 1-bromopropane with aqueous potassium hydroxide: ....

5 Formed by passing a mixture of ethene and steam under pressure over phosphoric acid on an inert support at 300 °C: ....

6 Formed when the vapour of J passes over hot aluminium oxide: ....

7 The compound that distils off on warming a mixture of C with an acidic solution of potassium dichromate(VI): ....

8 The product of heating F with excess acidic potassium dichromate(VI): ....

9 The main organic product of heating A under reflux with sodium bromide and concentrated sulfuric acid: ....

10 Formed on warming G and J in the presence of an acid catalyst: ....

11 Formed when F reacts with PCl$_5$: ....

12 Reacts with sodium giving off hydrogen, but does not react on heating with acidic potassium dichromate(VI): ....

A $CH_3—CH_2—CH_2—CH_2OH$

B $CH_3—CH_2—CHO$

C $CH_3—CH_2—CH_2OH$

D $CH_3—\underset{\underset{OH}{|}}{\overset{\overset{CH_3}{|}}{C}}—CH_3$

E $CH_3—O—CH_2—CH_3$

F $CH_3—CH_2—\underset{\overset{|}{OH}}{CH}—CH_3$

G $CH_3—C\overset{\overset{O}{\diagup\!\diagup}}{\diagdown_{OH}}$

H $CH_3—CH_2—CH_2—CH_2Br$

I $CH_3—CH_2—\overset{\overset{O}{||}}{C}—CH_3$

J $CH_3—CH_2OH$

K $CH_2{=}CH_2$

M $CH_3—CH_2—\underset{\overset{|}{Cl}}{CH}—CH_3$

N $CH_3—C\overset{\overset{O}{\diagup\!\diagup}}{\diagdown_{O—CH_2—CH_3}}$

Aldehydes^{A2}

Answer the questions and fill in the grid to reveal a word used to describe cyanide ions and other reagents that attack carbonyl groups in aldehydes.

1 The product of heating propan-1-ol with acidified potassium dichromate(VI) and distilling off the product as it forms.

2 Sodium tetrahydridoborate(III) is this type of reagent; it can convert aldehydes to alcohols.

3 The compound which adds to ethanal to form:

$$CH_3-\underset{\underset{OH}{|}}{\overset{\overset{H}{|}}{C}}-C\equiv N$$

4 The name of one reagent that can distinguish between aldehydes and ketones.

5 The colour of the solution of potassium dichromate(VI) after warming with excess of a primary alcohol.

6 The colour of a solution of potassium dichromate(VI).

7 The acid formed on heating propan-1-ol with excess acidified potassium dichromate(VI) under reflux.

8 The name of a blue solution that produces a brick-red precipitate on warming with ethanal.

9 The type of reaction when two molecules combine to form one product.

10 A characteristic of a C=O bond that arises from the high electronegativity of oxygen.

11 The action needed to purify a solid derivative before measuring its melting point.

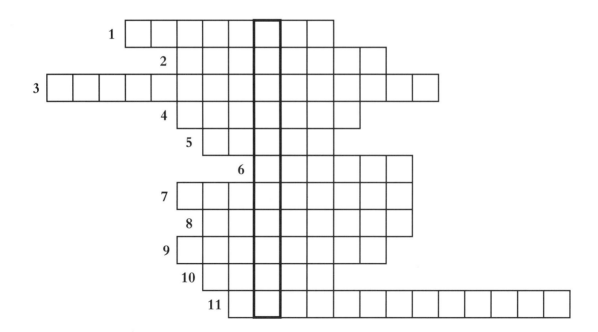

Alkanes[AS]

Name these structures.

```
    H   H   H
    |   |   |
H — C — C — C — H
    |   |   |
    H   |   H
    H — C — H
        |
        H
```

```
                H
                |
            H — C — H
    H   H   H   |   H
    |   |   |   |   |
H — C — C — C — C — C — H
    |   |   |   |   |
    H   |   H   H   H
    H — C — H
        |
        H
```

....

Annotate this diagram to explain why the boiling points of alkanes increase as the number of carbon atoms in the molecules increases.

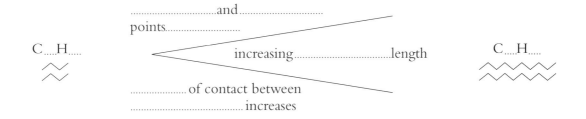

................................and...............................
points.............................

C....H....   increasing............................length   C....H....

.... of contact between
....increases

Complete this diagram to summarise the reactions of alkanes. The full diagram has the names and formulae of the organic products, the conditions for each reaction and the type of reaction.

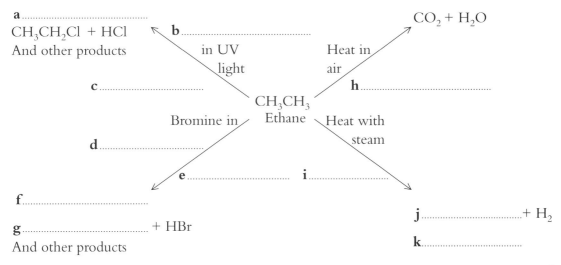

a..
$CH_3CH_2Cl + HCl$
And other products

b..

$CO_2 + H_2O$

in UV
light

Heat in
air

c..   **h**..

CH_3CH_3
Ethane

Bromine in   Heat with
steam

d..

e..   **i**..

f..

g.. $+ HBr$
And other products

j..$+ H_2$

k..

Alkenes[AS]

Name these structures.

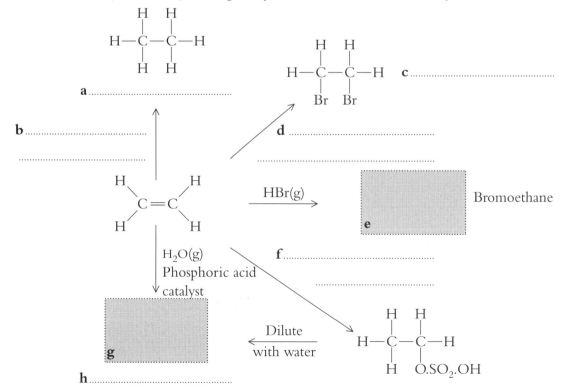

....

Label this diagram of an alkene molecule to distinguish σ and π bonds. Then state two different properties of alkenes that are related to the presence of double bonds in the molecules.

Property 1: ....

....

Property 2: ....

....

Complete this diagram to summarise the reactions of alkenes. The full diagram has the names and formulae of the organic products and the conditions for each reaction.

Aluminium extraction[AS]

Label this diagram of the apparatus used to extract aluminium by electrolysis. Label: a carbon anode, the cathode, the molten electrolyte, the molten metal formed. Then write equations for the electrode processes.

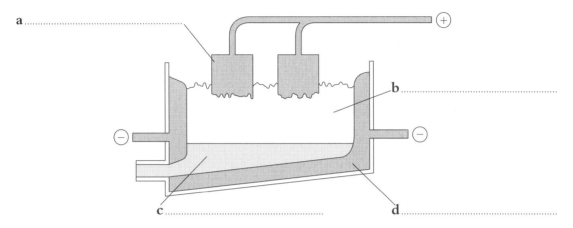

a...

b...

c... d...

At the anode: ....

At the cathode: ....

1   Why is the electrolyte a mixture of aluminium oxide and sodium hexafluoroaluminate(III) (cryolite)? ....

2   Why do the anodes have to be replaced regularly? ....

Amides[A2]

Give the name and structure of the organic products of these reactions.

1   The reaction of propanoyl chloride with ammonia.

2   The effect of reducing ethanamide with $LiAlH_4$ in ether and then adding water.

3   The product of heating ethanamide with P_2O_5.

4   The product of warming butanamide with bromine and concentrated potassium hydroxide solution.

Amines[A2]

ALKYL AMINES

Answer these questions about the reactions of primary amines.

1 Give the structure of the salt formed when hydrochloric acid reacts with butylamine.

2 Name the mechanism and type of reaction when ethylamine reacts with 1-bromopropane. ....

3 What are the four possible products when bromoethane reacts with ammonia? ....

ARYL AMINES

Complete this reaction sequence by filling in the missing structures, names, reagents and conditions.

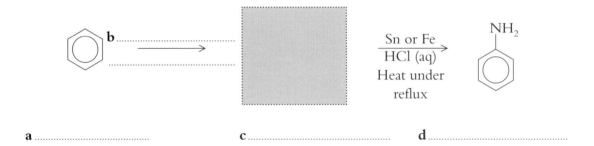

a ....   c ....   d ....

BASE STRENGTH

Annotate these diagrams to indicate the order of base strength of the three compounds.

$$C_3H_7 - \overset{\overset{\displaystyle H}{|}}{\underset{\displaystyle \cdot\cdot}{N}} - H \qquad\qquad H - \overset{\overset{\displaystyle H}{|}}{\underset{\displaystyle \cdot\cdot}{N}} - H$$

Propylamine   Ammonia   Phenylamine

Amino acids[A2]

Answer these questions.

1   Complete the structures of these two amino acids.

$$H_2N - \overset{|}{\underset{|}{C}} -$$ $$- \overset{|}{\underset{|}{\underset{H}{C}}} - CO_2H$$

    Glycine (aminoethanoic acid)   Alanine (2-aminopropanoic acid)

2   Explain why alanine has optical isomers while glycine does not.

    ....

    ....

3   Draw the structure of the zwitterion formed in a solution of alanine in water at pH 6 (its isoelectric point).

4   Draw the structure of the ion formed in an aqueous solution of alanine at:

    a   pH 2   **b**   pH 10

5   Draw the structures of the two possible dipeptides formed between glycine and alanine. In each structure label the peptide group.

Ammonia manufacture[AS]

Decide on the correct sequence for the parts of a flow diagram to describe the manufacture of ammonia. Write the four letters in the series of boxes.

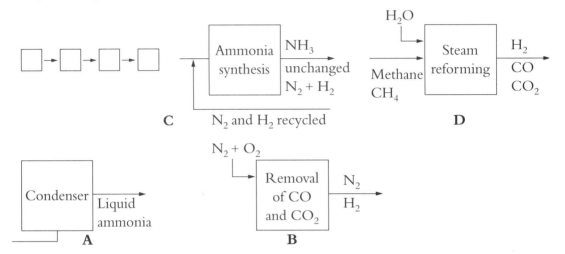

Select from the grid statements which help to explain the effect of pressure on the yield of ammonia and write the letters in a logical order. Then select from the grid statements which help to explain the effect of temperature on the yield of ammonia and write the letters in a logical order. (You may need to use a statement more than once.)

A So increasing the pressure increases the proportion of ammonia at equilibrium.	**B** So raising the temperature lowers the proportion of ammonia at equilibrium.
C There are 4 mol of gases on the left–hand side of the equation but only 2 mol on the right.	**D** The reaction is exothermic from left to right and so endothermic from right to on left.
E Le Chatelier's principle predicts that raising the temperature will make the position of equilibrium shift in the direction which takes in energy (tending to cool the mixture).	**F** The equilibrium system involved in ammonia manufacture is: $$N_2(g) + 3H_2(g) \rightleftharpoons 2NH_3(g)$$ $$\Delta H^{\ominus} = -92.4 \text{ kJ mol}^{-1}$$
G Le Chatelier's principle predicts that raising the pressure will make the equilibrium shift from left to right.	**H** This reduces the number of molecules and so tends to reduce the pressure.

Effect of pressure: ....

Effect of temperature: ....

Amounts of chemicals[AS]

Fill in the gaps in the sentence below. Then add the units to the formula and use it to answer the questions.

One mole is the amount of substance that contains as many atoms, molecules or ions as there are .... in exactly .... of the isotope carbon-12.

$$\text{Amount of substance}/\text{..........................} = \frac{\text{mass of substance}/\text{..........................}}{\text{molar mass}/\text{..........................}}$$

1   How many moles of:

    a   atoms are there in 2.0 g calcium? ....

    b   molecules are there in 5.0 g hydrogen fluoride? ....

    c   magnesium ions are there in 1.0 g magnesium oxide? ....

2   What is the mass of:

    a   2 mol calcium nitrate? ....

    b   0.05 mol ammonia? ....

    c   0.001 mol sodium hydroxide? ....

3   What is the amount in moles of:

    a   nitrate ions in 2 mol magnesium nitrate? ....

    b   nitrogen atoms in 1 mol ammonium sulfate? ....

    c   bromide ions in 0.5 mol barium bromide? ....

    d   aluminium ions in 0.1 mol aluminium sulfate? ....

4   Heating 4.68 g of a crystalline solid drove off water vapour leaving an anhydrous residue with a mass of 3.96 g. What amount of water, in moles, was driven off?

....

Aromatic hydrocarbons (arenes)^A2

Fill in the missing names a and c and the missing structure b.

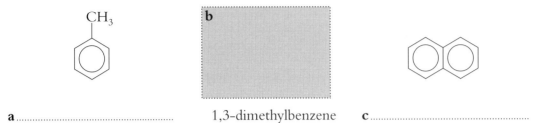

a ....
1,3-dimethylbenzene
c ....

The diagram shows the delocalised electrons in a benzene molecule. Give five properties of benzene which can be explained in terms of this model for the structure and bonding of benzene.

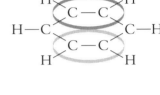

1 ....

2 ....

3 ....

4 ....

5 ....

Complete this diagram by writing the structures of the organic products of the electrophilic substitution reactions of benzene. Then name the products.

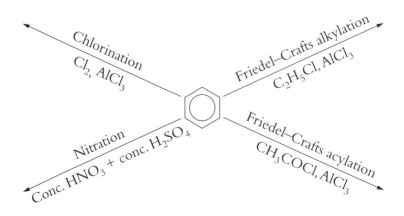

Arrhenius equation[A2]

Answer these questions about the Arrhenius equation, which in its logarithmic form is:

$$\ln k = \text{constant} = \frac{-E_a}{RT}$$

1   What do the symbols in the equation represent?

k ....

E_a ....

R ....

T ....

2   Indicate, in order, the key steps in using the equation to determine the activation energy for a reaction by experiment.

....

....

....

Avogadro constant[AS]

Answer the following questions given this value for the Avogadro constant, L.

$L = 6.02 \times 10^{23} \text{ mol}^{-1}$.

1   How many atoms are there in 0.02 mol of sulfur, S? ....

2   How many molecules are there in 0.02 mol of oxygen, O_2? ....

3   How many atoms are there in 12.0 g carbon-12? ....

4   How many molecules are there in 20.0 g hydrogen, H_2? ....

5   How many chloride ions are there in 0.75 mol calcium chloride, $CaCl_2$? ....

Balanced equations[AS]

Write the balanced symbol equation under each of these word equations. Include state symbols.

1   ethene + oxygen → carbon dioxide + water

    ....

2   ammonia + oxygen → nitrogen monoxide + steam

    ....

3   sodium + water → sodium hydroxide + hydrogen

    ....

4   chlorine + water → chloric(I) acid + hydrochloric acid

    ....

Benzene[A2]

Answer these questions about the structure and bonding in benzene.

1   Suggest two pieces of evidence which suggest that showing the molecule with alternating double and single bonds is misleading.

    ....

    ....

2   How many electrons are delocalised in a benzene molecule? ....

3   What is the evidence that benzene is more stable (by about 150 kJ mol^{-1}) than the Kekulé formula for the molecule suggests?

    ....

    ....

Bond breaking^{A2}

Add curly arrows to the diagrams below to distinguish between homolytic and heterolytic bond breaking.

$$Br\!-\!Br \;\rightarrow\; Br^{\bullet} \;+\; {}_{\bullet}Br \qquad\qquad H\!-\!Br \;\rightarrow\; H^{+} \;+\; Br^{-}$$

Indicate whether the bond breaking in these reactions is homolytic or heterolytic.

1   Reaction of chlorine with methane in ultraviolet light ....

2   Reaction of bromine with ethene ....

3   Reaction of aqueous hydroxide ions with 1-bromobutane ....

4   Catalytic cracking of hydrocarbons ....

5   Steam cracking of hydrocarbons ....

6   Polymerisation of ethene in the presence of a peroxide initiator ....

7   Reaction of hydrogen cyanide with propanone ....

8   Destruction of the ozone layer by CFCs ....

The equation below summarises the findings of a study of the hydrolysis of an ester with the oxygen atoms in the water labelled with an isotope of oxygen. What does this tell you about the bond breaking during this reaction?

....

....

....

Bond enthalpies[AS]

Use the table of average bond enthalpies to estimate the enthalpies of reaction for the changes in questions 1–4.

Bond	Average bond enthalpy/kJ mol^{-1}	Bond	Average bond enthalpy/kJ mol^{-1}
H–H	435	C–H	435
O–H	464	C–C	347
Cl–Cl	243	C=C	612
H–Cl	432	C=O	805
O=O	498	C–Cl	327

1   Hydrogen with chlorine to form two moles of hydrogen chloride ....

2   Propene with hydrogen to form propane ....

3   Methane with chlorine to form chloromethane ....

4   Methane burning in oxygen to form carbon dioxide and steam ....

Bond lengths[A2]

What generalisations can be made about the carbon–carbon bond lengths in these diagrams.

....

....

Born–Haber cycle[A2]

Match the terms in the left-hand column with their definitions in the right-hand column by drawing in lines to link each number to the appropriate letter.

Term			*Definition*	
Enthalpy change of atomisation	1		A	The standard enthalpy change when one mole of an ionic compound forms from free gaseous ions.
Electron affinity	2		B	The energy needed to remove one mole of electrons from one mole of gaseous atoms.
Lattice enthalpy	3		C	The enthalpy change when 1 mol of gaseous atoms of an element gains electrons to become negative ions.
First ionisation energy	4		D	The enthalpy change to produce one mole of gaseous atoms from an element.

Identify the enthalpy changes ΔH_1 to ΔH_6 in the diagram. Then calculate the lattice enthalpy for calcium chloride.

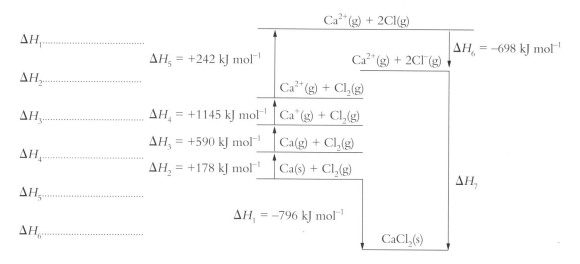

Bromine extraction[AS]

The extraction of bromine from sea water is a four-stage process. Match the stages with the four descriptions by drawing lines to connect each number to the appropriate letter. Then write balanced equations for the chemical changes in stages 1, 3 and 4.

Stage			*Description*
Oxidation of bromide ions to bromine	**1**	**A**	The solution flows down a tower with a flow of chlorine gas and steam passing up it. Bromine evaporates in the steam. The mixture of steam and bromine is cooled and condensed, producing a dense lower bromine layer under a layer of water.
Separation of bromine vapour	**2**	**B**	The air with bromine vapour meets sulfur dioxide gas and a fine mist of water. The sulfur dioxide turns into sulfate ions. After this stage, the concentration of bromine in the solution is 1500 times greater than in sea water.
Formation of hydrobromic acid	**3**	**C**	A blast of air through the reaction mixture carries away the product and helps to concentrate it.
Displacement and purification of bromine	**4**	**D**	Sea water is filtered and acidified to pH 3.5 to prevent chlorine and bromine reacting with water. Then chlorine is added to the solution.

Stage 1 equation: ....

Stage 3 equation: ....

Stage 4 equation: ....

List three important uses of bromine:

1 ....

2 ....

3 ....

Brønsted–Lowry theory[A2]

Answer question 1–14 by writing the letters for the appropriate structures in the spaces provided. You can use a symbol or structure more than once. There may be more than one possible correct answer.

1   The symbol for a proton ....

2   A representation of an oxonium ion ....

3   A chemical species with a dative covalent bond ....

4   A proton donor ....

5   A proton acceptor ....

6   A chemical species which can act both as a proton acceptor and a proton donor ....

7   A monoprotic acid ....

8   A diprotic acid ....

9   The conjugate base of ethanoic acid ....

10   The conjugate acid of ammonia ....

11   A strong acid ....

12   A weak acid ....

13   A strong base ....

14   A weak base ....

HCl
a

OH^-
b

$CH_3CO_2^-$
c

HCO_3^-
d

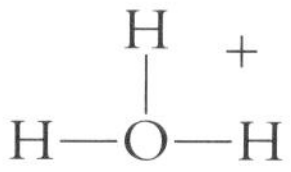

$\begin{array}{c} H \\ | \\ H-O-H \end{array}^+$
e

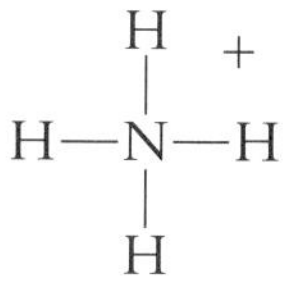

$\begin{array}{c} H \\ | \\ H-N-H \\ | \\ H \end{array}^+$
f

H_2SO_4
g

NH_3
h

H^+
i

O^{2-}
j

CH_3CO_2H
k

Buffer solutions[A2]

The left-hand column has the first part of a series of sentences. The right-hand column has the phrases that complete these sentences. Match the beginnings and endings to create accurate statements about buffer solutions. In each case draw a line from the letter to the matching number.

Beginnings

Buffer solutions are mixtures of molecules and ions in solution ...... **A**

Chemists use buffers ...... **B**

The pH of blood is closely controlled ...... **C**

A typical buffer mixture consists of ...... **D**

Buffers are equilibrium systems ...... **E**

If the concentrations of the weak acid and its salt are the same ...... **F**

The pH of a buffer mixture can be calculated ...... **G**

Diluting a buffer solution with water ...... **H**

Endings

1 ...... the pH of the buffer is equal to pK_a for the acid.

2 ...... by buffers within the narrow range 7.38 to 7.42.

3 ...... when they want to investigate chemical reactions at a fixed pH.

4 ...... does not change the ratio of the concentrations of the salt and acid so the pH does not change.

5 ...... which illustrate the practical importance of Le Chatelier's principle.

6 ...... from the formula $pH = pK_a + \lg [salt]/[acid]$

7 ...... which help to keep the pH more or less constant.

8 ...... a solution of a weak acid and one of its salts.

What is the pH of a buffer solution containing $0.50 \ mol \ dm^{-3}$ ethanoic acid and $1.00 \ mol \ dm^{-3}$ sodium ethanoate? The pK_a of ethanoic acid is 4.8.

....

Carbonyl compounds[A2]

Fill in the missing symbols or words in these sentences.

Carbonyl compounds contain the .... group.

The two main classes of carbonyl compounds are the .... and the ....

The carbon–oxygen double bond is .... with the electrons drawn towards the more .... oxygen atom.

The characteristic reactions of carbonyl compounds are .... reactions and addition–elimination reactions.

Carboxylic acids[A2]

Complete this chart by adding missing formulae, naming the organic products and adding the reagents and conditions for the reaction beside the arrows.

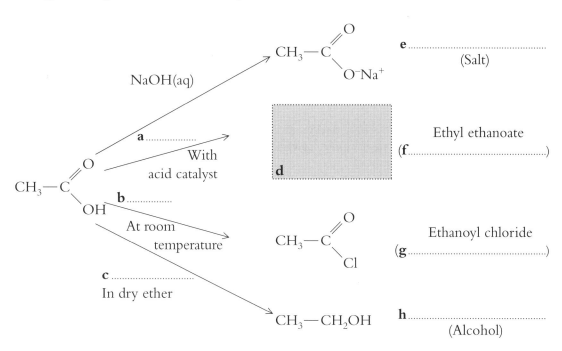

Catalysts[AS]

Match the catalysts in the left-hand column with the processes for which they are used in the right-hand column. Draw lines to connect the items which match.

A	Iron	**1**	Cracking of hydrocarbons
B	Nickel	**2**	Conversion of SO_2 to SO_3
C	Zeolite	**3**	Synthesis of NH_3 from H_2 and N_2
D	Platinum/rhodium	**4**	Oxidation of NH_3 to NO
E	Vanadium(v) oxide	**5**	Hydrogenation of C=C bonds

Label the axes of this graph. Then annotate the graph with these words and phrases: reactants, products, activation energy with catalyst, activation energy without catalyst.

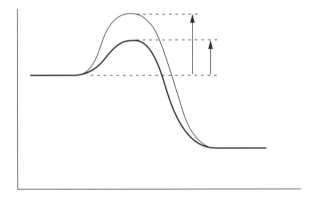

Label the axes of this graph. Then annotate the graph with these phrases: activation energy with catalyst, activation energy without catalyst. Shade two areas: one to show the number of molecules able to react in the absence of a catalyst and the other to show the number of molecules able to react with a catalyst.

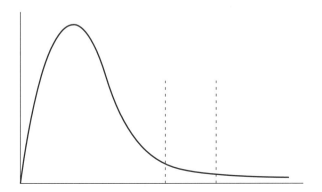

Catalytic converter[AS]

Complete this table to show the pollutant gases from car engines and their effects.

Pollutant	Origin of the pollutant
Carbon dioxide, CO_2	Complete combustion of hydrocarbons in petrol
a	Incomplete combustion of fuel
Hydrocarbons, C_xH_y	c ....
b	Reaction of nitrogen and oxygen from the air in the hot engine

Complete this diagram to show the gases which leave a catalytic converter.

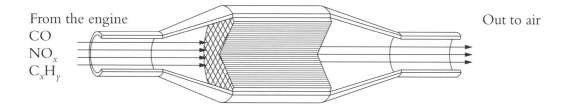

From the engine
CO
NO_x
C_xH_y

Out to air

Changes of state[AS]

Label each box with the state it represents, then label the arrows in the diagram with the name of the change of state. Indicate whether the change is exothermic or endothermic. Then, below each of the three boxes, describe briefly the arrangement and movement of the particles in each state.

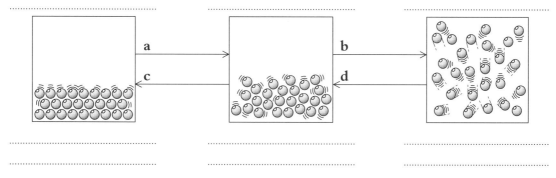

....

a

c

b

d

....

....

Chelates[A2]

The grid of letters describes what is special about these complex ions. Read the rows from left to right and from top to bottom. Three or four letters have been missed out of each row. There are no spaces between words and there is no punctuation. Fill in the missing letters. Find the word breaks. Put in the punctuation. Learn about chelates.

C	H	E	L	□	T	E	S	A	□	E	C	O	M	□	L	E	X
I	O	N	□	I	N	W	H	□	C	H	E	A	□	H	L	I	G
A	N	□	F	O	R	M	□	M	O	R	E	□	H	A	N	O	□
E	□	A	T	I	V	□	C	O	V	A	□	E	N	T	B	□	N
□	W	I	T	H	□	C	E	N	T	□	A	L	M	E	□	A	L
I	O	N	C	□	E	L	A	T	□	S	A	R	E	□	O	R	M
E	D	B	□	B	I	D	E	□	T	A	T	E	□	N	D	P	O
L	Y	□	E	N	T	A	□	E	L	I	G	□	N	D	S	S	□
C	□	A	S	E	D	□	A	C	H	E	□	A	T	E	S	□	R
□	U	S	U	A	□	L	Y	M	O	□	E	S	T	A	□	L	E
T	H	A	N	□	O	M	P	L	□	X	E	S	W	□	T	H	M
O	N	O	□	E	N	T	A	□	E	L	I	G	□	N	D	S	■

Chiral compounds[A2]

Identify the molecules which are chiral by using an asterisk to indicate the asymmetric centres in these molecules.

A

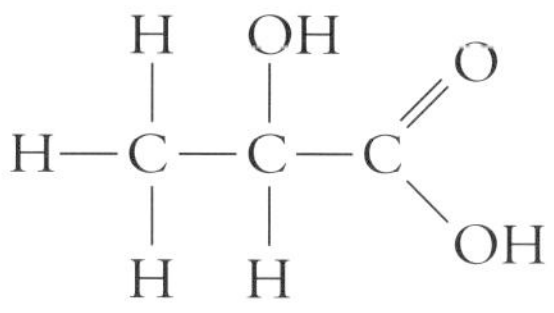

B

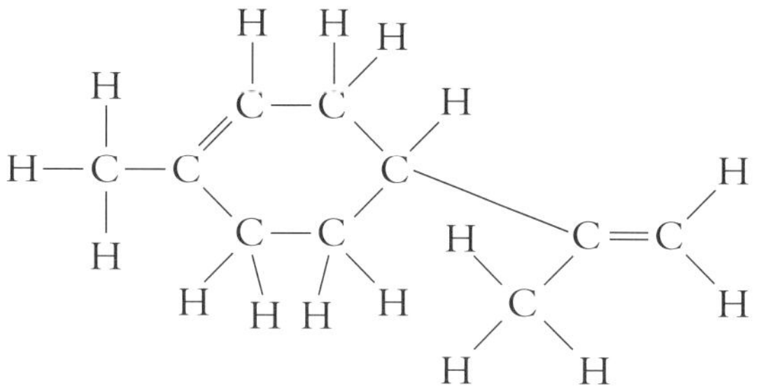

C

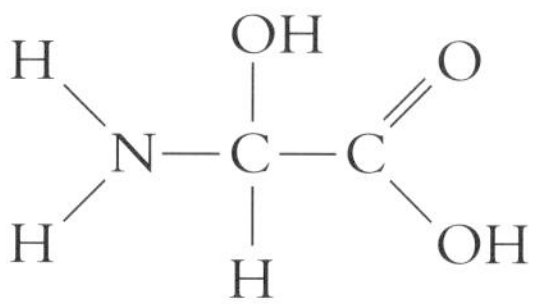

D

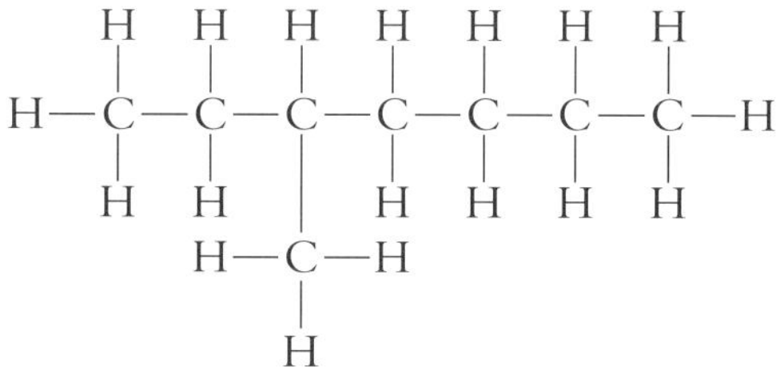

Draw a representation of the three-dimensional shape of the two mirror image forms of any one chiral compound.

What is the main difference in the properties of the mirror image forms of a chiral compound?

....

....

Give one reason why chirality is important in living things.

....

....

Chlorine^AS

Complete this diagram to summarise the reactions of chlorine.

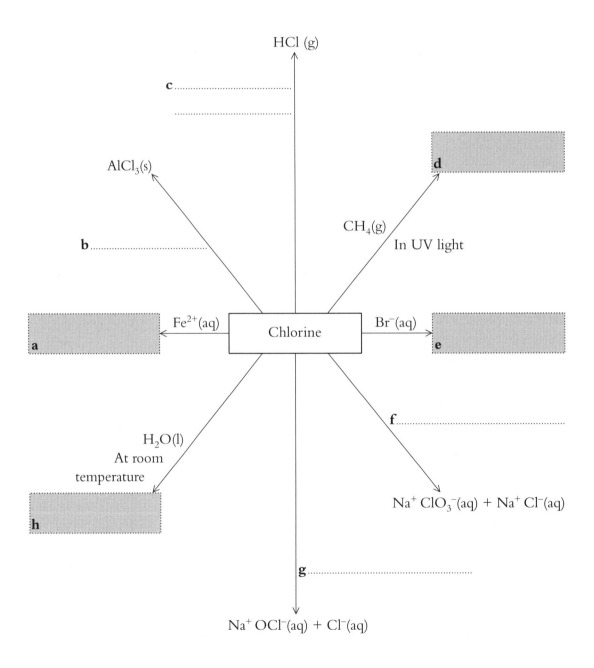

HCl (g)

c ....

....

AlCl₃(s)

d

b ....

CH₄(g)

In UV light

Fe²⁺(aq)   Chlorine   Br⁻(aq)

a   e

f ....

H₂O(l)

At room

temperature

Na⁺ ClO₃⁻(aq) + Na⁺ Cl⁻(aq)

h

g ....

Na⁺ OCl⁻(aq) + Cl⁻(aq)

Complex ions^{A2}

Answer questions 1–12 by writing the letters for any appropriate formulae or structures in the spaces provided. There may be more than one correct answer for a question. You can use a formula or structure more than once.

1   The diammine silver(I) ion ....

2   The tetrachlorocuprate(II) ion ....

3   The complex in which the metal ion is in oxidation state +3 ....

4   A complex in which all the ligands are negative ions ....

5   A complex in which is pale pink in aqueous solution ....

6   A complex with a bidentate ligand ....

7   A complex with a hexadentate ligand ....

8   A linear complex ....

9   A complex with an octahedral shape ....

10 A complex with a deep red colour formed during a chemical test for the metal ion ....

11 A complex used to treat some forms of cancer ....

12 A complex formed when 'fixing' photographic negatives or prints ....

A $[Co(H_2O)_6]^{2+}$ **B** $[Ag(NH_3)_2]^+$

C $[Fe(H_2O)_5(SCN)]^{2+}$

D $[Ag(S_2O_3)_2]^{3-}$

E $[CuCl_4]^{2-}$

F
$$\left[\begin{array}{c} Cl \qquad NH_3 \\ Pt \\ Cl \qquad NH_3 \end{array} \right]$$

G
$$\left[\begin{array}{c} H_2N{-}CH_2 \\ CH_2 \\ \overset{H_2}{N} \qquad NH_2 \\ H_2C \\ H_2C \qquad Ni \\ NH_2 \qquad NH_2 \\ CH_2 \\ H_2N{-}CH_2 \end{array} \right]^{2+}$$

H
$$\left[\begin{array}{c} O{=}C{-}O \\ O{=}C{-}CH_2 \quad CH_2 \\ O \qquad N \\ CH_2 \\ Cu \qquad CH_2 \\ O{-}C{-}H_2C \quad N \\ O \qquad CH_2 \\ O{-}C \\ O \end{array} \right]^{2-}$$

J
$$\left[\begin{array}{c} NC \quad \overset{CN}{} \quad CN \\ Fe \\ NC \quad \underset{CN}{} \quad CN \end{array} \right]^{4-}$$

I
$$\left[\begin{array}{c} Cl \\ Co \\ Cl \qquad Cl \\ Cl \end{array} \right]^{2-}$$

31

Concentrations[AS]

Work out the concentration in moles per litre of these solutions.

1   A solution with 0.002 mol ammonia, NH_3, in 50 cm^3 solution ....

2   A solution with 10.0 g NaOH in 250 cm^3 solution ....

3   A solution with 4.25 g $AgNO_3$ in 200 cm^3 solution ....

What amount, in moles, of the named compound is there in the following?

4   A 0.5 dm^3 sample of 2.0 mol dm^{-3} potassium hydroxide solution ....

5   A 25 cm^3 sample of 0.5 mol dm^{-3} potassium iodide solution ....

6   A 5 cm^3 sample of 0.01 mol dm^{-3} dilute hydrochloric acid ....

Condensation polymerisation[A2]

Fill in the missing words in these sentences.

A condensation reaction is a reaction in which molecules join together by splitting off a small .... such as .... The formation of an ....from an acid and an alcohol is a condensation reaction.

Condensation polymers are produced by a series of condensation reactions splitting off a small molecule such as water between the functional groups of the .... Where each monomer has two functional groups, this type of polymerisation produces .... Examples of condensation polymers are .... such as nylon and ....

Condensation polymers make good fibres because they form long straight-chain molecules with few side chains and with relatively .... intermolecular forces between .... bonds in neighbouring chains.

Corrosion[A2]

Answer the questions about the diagram to show the chemical changes in a droplet of water on a piece of iron.

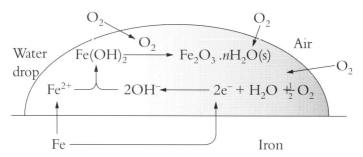

1   Which two chemical species are oxidised? ....

2   Which chemical species is reduced? ....

3   Which formula represents rust? ....

4   Which region of the metal surface is anodic? ....

5   Which region of the metal surface is cathodic? ....

Covalent bonding[AS]

Draw in dots and crosses to show the shared pairs and lone pairs of electrons in these molecules all with single covalent bonds.

		H		H		Cl
F F		H O		H N H		Cl C Cl
						Cl

Draw in dots and crosses to show the shared pairs and lone pairs of electrons in these molecules all with multiple covalent bonds

				H	H
O O	N N	O C O		C	C
				H	H

Covalent giant structures[AS]

Give two examples of materials with covalent giant structures.

....

....

Fill in the gaps in this table to show how the properties of materials with covalent giant structures can be explained in terms of structure and bonding.

Property	Explanation
High melting and boiling points	c
a	Covalent bonds are strong and have a definite length and direction
b	In most covalent bonds the electrons are fixed and cannot move. An exception is d.................. which has delocalised electrons
Insoluble in water and organic solvents	e

Covalent molecular structures[AS]

Give three examples of elements with covalent molecular structures.

....

....

....

Give three examples of compounds with covalent molecular structures.

....

....

....

Fill in the gaps in this table to show how the properties of materials with covalent molecular structures can be explained in terms of structure and bonding.

Property	Explanation
a	The forces between the molecules are weak
Non-conductors of electricity when solid and when liquid	c
b	Non-polar molecules cannot break into the hydrogen-bonded structure of water, but can mix freely with other non-polar molecules
Soluble in water if highly polar or with atoms that can form hydrogen bonds	d

Dative covalent bonding^AS

Sketch simple diagrams to show how dative covalent bonding accounts for the formation of: an ammonium ion and an oxonium ion.

Delocalisation of electrons^A2

Put a tick against any of the following phenomena which are associated with delocalised electrons. Put a cross against any which are not.

1   The conduction of electricity by metals ....

2   The conduction of electricity by graphite ....

3   The conduction of electricity by molten sodium chloride ....

4   The low density of ice ....

5   The tetrahedral shape of a methane molecule ....

6   The planar shape of a nitrate ion ....

7   The acidity of ethanoic acid ....

8   The base strength of an ammonia molecule ....

9   The stability of benzene ....

10   The colour of methyl orange ....

Diazonium salts[A2]

The left-hand column has the first parts of a series of sentences. The right-hand column has the phrases which complete these sentences. Match the beginnings and endings to create accurate statements about diazonium salts. In each case draw a line from the letter to the matching number.

Beginnings

Diazonium salts form when aryl amines, such as phenylamine, ...   **A**

Adding dilute hydrochloric to a solution of ......   **B**

Benzene diazonium chloride consists of ......   **C**

Diazonium salts are unstable so ......   **D**

Above 10 °C ......   **E**

The commercial importance of ......   **F**

A coupling reaction links together ......   **G**

Diazonium salts are also useful intermediates which ......   **H**

Endings

1   ...... sodium nitrite produces a solution of nitrous acid.

2   ...... they are made as needed in solution and kept cold.

3   ...... diazonium salts is based on their coupling reactions to form azo dyes.

4   ...... two aromatic (arene) rings with a —N=N— group.

5   ...... react with nitrous acid, HNO_2, below about 10 °C.

6   ...... benzene diazonium chloride begin to decompose to phenol and nitrogen.

7   ...... make it possible to make derivatives of arenes.

8   ...... a benzene ring linked to a —$N_2^+Cl^-$ group.

Disproportionation[AS/A2]

Use oxidation numbers to decide whether or not these changes are disproportionation reactions and, where they are, to identify the element which disproportionates.

1   $Cl_2(aq) + H_2O(l) \rightarrow HOCl(aq) + H^+(aq) + Cl^-(aq)$ ....

2   $2S_2O_3^{2-}(aq) + I_2(aq) \rightarrow S_4O_6^{2-}(aq) + 2I^-(aq)$ ....

3   $2H_2O_2(aq) \rightarrow 2H_2O(l) + O_2(g)$ ....

Electrochemical cells[A2]

Label this diagram to include concentrations, temperature and pressure for this apparatus which has been set up to measure the standard electrode potential of zinc.

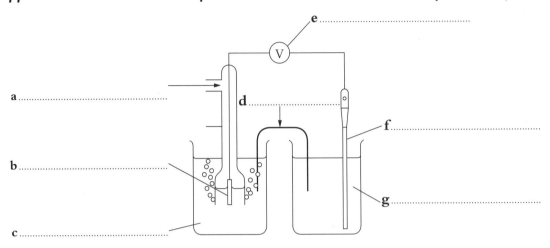

Answer these questions.

1 What is the standard electrode potential of the right-hand electrode in each of these cells?

a $Pt[H_2(g)] | 2H^+(aq) \: \| \: Cd^{2+}(aq) | Cd(s)$ $E_{cell}^{\ominus} = -0.40\,V$ ....

b $Pt[H_2(g)] | 2H^+(aq) \: \| \: Ag^+(aq) | Ag(s)$ $E_{cell}^{\ominus} = +0.80\,V$ ....

c $Pt[H_2(g)] | 2H^+(aq) \: \| \: Br_2(aq), 2Br^-(s) | Pt$ $E_{cell}^{\ominus} = +1.09\,V$ ....

2 Use your answers to question **1** to work out the cell emfs of these cells:

a $Cd(s) | Cd^{2+}(aq) \: \| \: Ag^+(aq) | Ag(s)$ $E_{cell}^{\ominus} = $ V

b $Ag(s) | Ag^+(aq) \: \| \: Br_2(aq), 2Br^-(aq) | Pt$ $E_{cell}^{\ominus} = $ V

c $Pt | 2Br^-(aq), Br_2(aq) \: \| \: Cd^{2+}(aq) | Cd(s)$ $E_{cell}^{\ominus} = $ V

3 Write ionic equations for any reactions which you would expect to tend to happen, based on the information in question **2**.

....

....

....

Electrode potentials[A2]

This electrochemical series is based on a selection of standard electrode potentials. Here the most negative electrode potential is at the top of the series and the most positive electrode system at the bottom. Answer the question by referring to these electrode potentials.

Half-cell	Half-reaction	$E^{\ominus}/V$
$Mg^{2+}(aq)\,|\,Mg(s)$	$Mg^{2+}(aq) + 2e^- \rightleftharpoons Mg(s)$	-2.37
$Zn^{2+}(aq)\,|\,Zn(s)$	$Zn^{2+}(aq) + 2e^- \rightleftharpoons Zn(s)$	-0.76
$Fe^{2+}(aq)\,|\,Fe(s)$	$Fe^{2+}(aq) + 2e^- \rightleftharpoons Fe(s)$	-0.44
$V^{3+}(aq)\,|\,V^{2+}(aq)$	$V^{3+}(aq) + 2e^- \rightleftharpoons V^{2+}(aq)$	-0.26
$Cu^{2+}(aq)\,|\,Cu(s)$	$Cu^{2+}(aq) + 2e^- \rightleftharpoons Cu(s)$	$+0.34$
$I_2(aq),2I^-(aq)\,|\,Pt$	$I_2(aq) + 2e^- \rightleftharpoons 2I^-(aq)$	$+0.54$
$Fe^{3+}(aq),Fe^{2+}(aq)\,|\,Pt$	$Fe^{3+}(aq) + e^- \rightleftharpoons Fe^{2+}(aq)$	$+0.77$
$Cl_2(aq),2Cl^-(aq)\,|\,Pt$	$Cl_2(aq) + 2e^- \rightleftharpoons 2Cl^-(aq)$	$+1.36$

1 Which is the strongest reducing agent in the table? ....

2 Which is the strongest oxidising agent in the table? ....

3 Predict which of these species will tend to react with each other. Write ionic equations for any reactions you would expect to take place:

 a iron(III) ions and iodide ions in aqueous solution ....

 b magnesium metal with aqueous copper(II) ions ....

 c copper metal with aqueous magnesium ions ....

 d iron(III) ions in aqueous solution with metallic iron ....

 e aqueous vanadium(III) ions and metallic zinc ....

 f vanadium(III) ions and chloride ions in aqueous solution ....

Electrolysis of brine[AS]

Complete the labelling of this diagram which illustrates the process used to manufacture chlorine and other chemicals from brine.

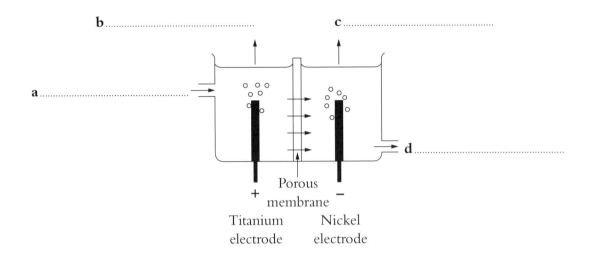

b ....   c ....

a ....

d ....

\+   Porous
membrane   −

Titanium   Nickel
electrode   electrode

1   Write equations for the electrode processes during the electrolysis of brine.

     At the anode: ....

     At the cathode: ....

2   Give two uses of each of the products:

     Chlorine: ....

     Sodium hydroxide: ....

     Hydrogen: ....

Electron configurations^{AS}

Complete the three statements which are the rules governing the way that electrons fill the energy levels in atoms.

- An electron goes into the .... available energy level.

- Each orbital can only hold .... electrons.

- Where there are two or more orbitals at the same .... they each take one electron with parallel ...., before the electrons pair up.

Using little arrows to represent the electrons, complete the three diagrams below to show the electron configurations of the named elements.

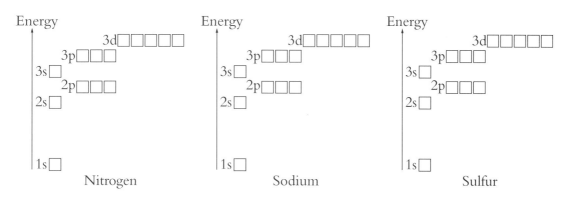

The electron configuration of boron is $1s^2 2s^2 2p^1$. Write out the electron configurations of the following elements in this style.

Potassium: ....

Magnesium: ....

Fluorine: ....

Chlorine: ....

Electrophilic addition[AS/A2]

Complete these statements.

1   Electrophilic addition is characteristic of ....

2   Examples of electrophiles which can add to these compounds are

....

3   Bond breaking during electrophilic addition is h .... lytic.

4   Curly arrows in a reaction mechanism show ....

5   A carbocation is an .... that forms during organic reactions in which

carbon atom carries a .... charge

Electrophilic substitution^{AS/A2}

Answer these questions about the bromination of benzene, which is an example of electrophilic substitution.

1   Complete this equation by showing the products on the right-hand side to show why iron(III) bromide is a catalyst for the reaction.

$$
\begin{array}{c}
\text{Br} \\
| \\
\text{Br—Fe} \qquad \text{Br—Br} \longrightarrow \\
| \\
\text{Br}
\end{array}
$$

2   Which is the electrophile for the bromination of bromine? ....

3   Another possible catalyst is aluminium chloride. What are the chemical similarities between iron(III) bromide and aluminium chloride that mean that they can both be catalysts for this process?

    ....

4   a   Complete this summary of the mechanism of electrophilic bromination of benzene. Show the interaction of a benzene molecule and the electrophile on the left and the products on the right.

    b   Why does an alternative second step (addition of a bromide ion as in electrophilic addition to alkenes) not happen with benzene?

    ....

43

Empirical formula[AS]

Complete this worked example with the help of data from the Periodic table on page viii.

Example: Analysis of an organic compound shows that it consists of 38.7% carbon by mass combined with 9.7% hydrogen. What is the empirical formula of the compound? (Assume that the rest of the compound consists of oxygen.)

ANSWER

	Carbon	Hydrogen	Oxygen
Combining masses in 100 g	38.7 g	9.7 g	.... g
Molar masses of elements	.... g mol^{-1}	1 g mol^{-1}	.... g mol^{-1}
Amounts combined	$\dfrac{38.7\,\text{g}}{...........\ \text{g mol}^{-1}}$ = ...mol	$\dfrac{...........\ \text{g}}{1\,\text{g mol}^{-1}}$ = ...mol	$\dfrac{...........\ \text{g}}{...........\ \text{g mol}^{-1}}$ = ...mol

Simplest ratio of amounts   ....

The formula is C....H....O....

Now work out the empirical (simplest) formula for these examples:

a   A chloride of copper consisting of 64.1% copper and 35.9% chlorine.

....

b   A compound containing 62.5% lead, 8.5% nitrogen and 29.0% oxygen.

....

c   An amino acid consisting of 32.12% carbon, 6.71% hydrogen, 18.59% nitrogen and 42.58% oxygen.

....

Enthalpy changes^{AS}

Match the names of the enthalpy changes in column 1 with the definitions in column 2 by drawing lines to connect each number to the appropriate letter.

Enthalpy change

Definition

The standard enthalpy change of a reaction **1**

A The enthalpy change of reaction when amounts of an acid and an alkali (as shown in the chemical equation) react under standard conditions.

The standard enthalpy change of neutralisation **2**

B The enthalpy change when one mole of the compound forms from its elements under standard conditions with the elements and the compound in their standard states.

The standard enthalpy change of combustion of a substance, $\Delta H_{c,298}^{\ominus}$ **3**

C The enthalpy change on breaking one mole of a particular covalent bond in a gaseous molecule.

The standard enthalpy change of formation of a compound, $\Delta H_{f,298}^{\ominus}$ **4**

D The enthalpy change when the amounts shown in the chemical equation react under standard conditions with the reactants and products in their standard states.

The bond dissociation enthalpy **5**

E The enthalpy change when one mole of the substance completely burns in oxygen under standard conditions with the reactants and products in their standard states.

What are the conditions for measuring or calculating standard enthalpy changes:

● temperature ....

● pressure ....

Enthalpy change of formation^{AS}

Complete this Hess's law cycle to calculate a value for the standard enthalpy change of formation of ethene given these values for standard enthalpy changes of combustion.

$$\Delta H_c^{\ominus} [C_2H_4(g)] = -1411 \text{ kJ mol}^{-1} \quad \Delta H_c^{\ominus} [C(s)] = -394 \text{ kJ mol}^{-1}$$

$$\Delta H_c^{\ominus} [H_2(g)] = -286 \text{ kJ mol}^{-1}$$

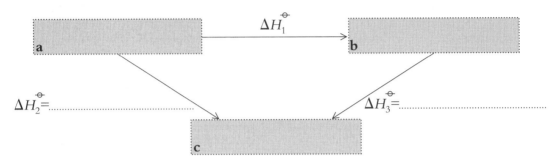

$$\Delta H_f^{\ominus} [C_2H_4] = \text{.............. kJ mol}^{-1}$$

Enthalpy change of reaction^{AS}

Complete this Hess's law cycle to calculate a value for the standard enthalpy change of reaction of ethene with steam to form ethanol given these values for standard enthalpy changes of formation.

$$\Delta H_f^{\ominus} [C_2H_4(g)] = +51 \text{ kJ mol}^{-1} \quad \Delta H_f^{\ominus} [H_2O(g)] = -242 \text{ kJ mol}^{-1}$$

$$\Delta H_f^{\ominus} [C_2H_5OH(l)] = -277 \text{ kJ mol}^{-1}$$

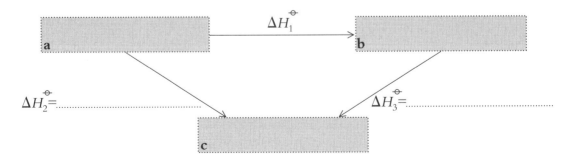

$$C_2H_4(g) + H_2O(g) \rightarrow C_2H_5OH(l) \quad \Delta H^{\ominus} = \text{.............. kJ mol}^{-1}$$

Enthalpy change of solution^{A2}

Fill in the blanks in the statements below. Use the information to complete the labelling of the enthalpy level diagram. Then calculate a value for the enthalpy change of solution of sodium chloride.

The enthalpy change of solution is the enthalpy change when .... of a substance dissolves in a stated amount of water under .... conditions.

The enthalpy change of solution is the .... between the energy needed to separate the ions from the crystal lattice (− lattice enthalpy) and the energy given out as the ions are .... (sum of the hydration enthalpies).

$$\Delta H^{\ominus}_{solution} = \Delta H^{\ominus}_{hydration\ cation} + \Delta H^{\ominus}_{hydration\ anion} - \Delta H^{\ominus}_{lattice}$$

b .... + **c** ....

$-\Delta H^{\ominus}_{lattice} = +\ 788\text{kJ mol}^{-1}$

$\Delta H^{\ominus}_{hydration\ Na^+} + \Delta H^{\ominus}_{hydration\ Cl^-}$
$= -784 \text{ kJ mol}^{-1}$

$Na^+(aq) + Cl^-(aq)$

a .... + aq $\quad \Delta H^{\ominus}_{solution}$

$NaCl(s) + aq \rightarrow$ .... + ... $\quad \Delta H^{\ominus}_{solution} =$ .... kJ mol^{-1}

The enthalpy change of solution is a small difference between two .... enthalpy changes.

The lattice and the hydration enthalpies tend to be affected in the same way by changes in the sizes of the ions and their charges.

The smaller the ions and the larger the charges the .... the lattice enthalpy but also the larger the sum of the enthalpy changes when the ions are ....

Entropy[A2]

The left-hand column has the first part of a series of sentences. The right-hand column has the phrases which complete these sentences. Match the beginnings and endings to create accurate statements about entropy changes. In each case draw a line from the letter to the matching number.

Beginnings

Entropy change, ΔS, is a thermo-chemical quantity which **1**

Change happens in the direction which **2**

The total entropy change is the sum of **3**

The entropy of a system measures the number of ways, W, of arranging **4**

Gases generally have higher entropies than liquids which **5**

The entropy change of the surroundings **6**

Endings

A ......the molecules and sharing out the energy between the molecules.

B ...... the entropy change of the system and the entropy change of the surroundings
$$\Delta S_{total} = \Delta S_{system} + \Delta S_{surroundings}$$

C ...... have higher entropies than solids.

D ......makes it possible to predict the direction of changes.

E ...... is determined by the size of the enthalpy change, ΔH, and the temperature, T in Kelvin.
$$\Delta S_{surroundings} = -\,\Delta H/T$$

F ...... leads to a total increase in entropy.

Enzymes[A2]

Fill in the blanks in these sentences.

Enzymes are .... molecules which are the .... for biochemical reactions. Saliva contains the enzyme amylase which aids digestion by speeding up the .... of starch to a sugar. Each enzyme catalyses a particular .... Each enzyme works best at a particular .... and ....

Esters[A2]

Label the ester links in these structures. The structures show: a fat, aspirin, a fruit flavour and a polyester. Label the structures to show which is which.

A

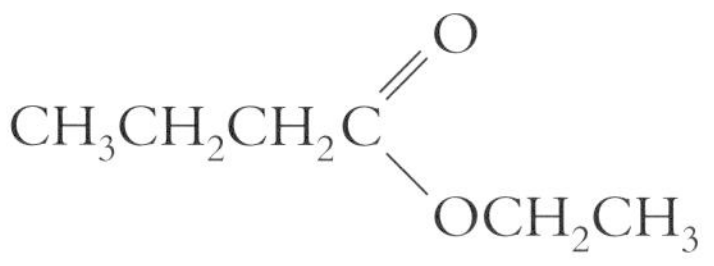

$$CH_3CH_2CH_2C \overset{\displaystyle O}{\underset{\displaystyle OCH_2CH_3}{\diagdown}}$$

C

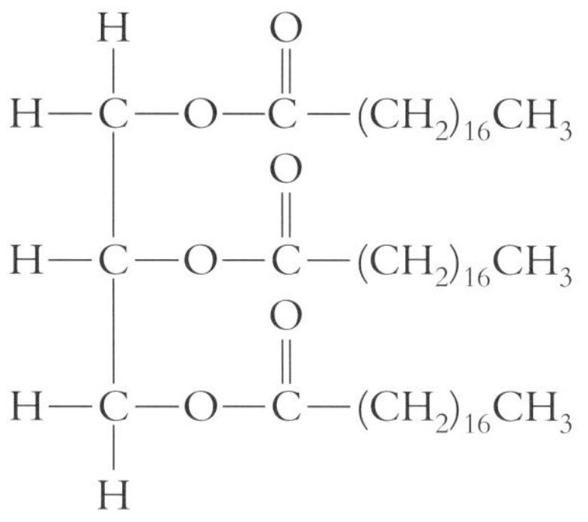

$$H-\overset{\displaystyle H}{\underset{\displaystyle |}{C}}-O-\overset{\displaystyle O}{\overset{\displaystyle ||}{C}}-(CH_2)_{16}CH_3$$
$$H-\overset{\displaystyle |}{C}-O-\overset{\displaystyle O}{\overset{\displaystyle ||}{C}}-(CH_2)_{16}CH_3$$
$$H-\overset{\displaystyle |}{\underset{\displaystyle H}{C}}-O-\overset{\displaystyle O}{\overset{\displaystyle ||}{C}}-(CH_2)_{16}CH_3$$

B

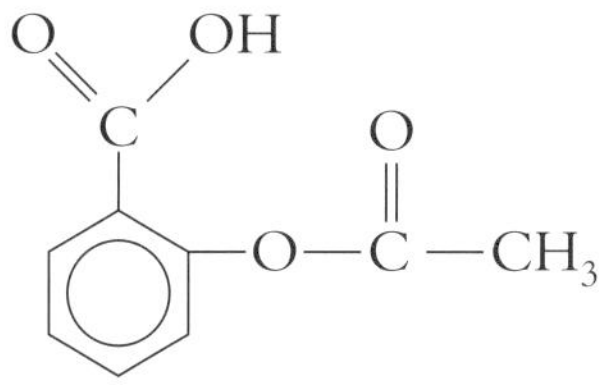

D

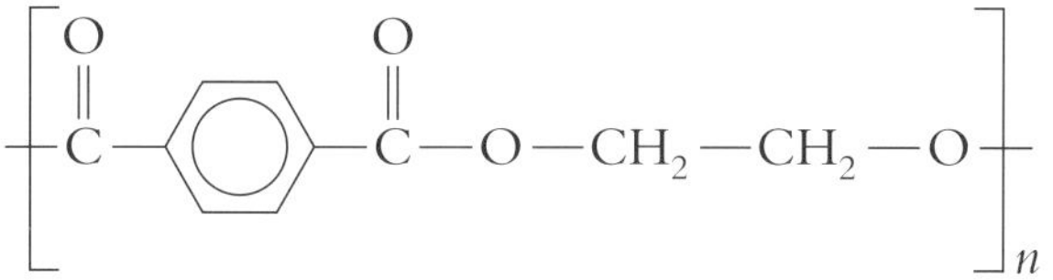

Complete these two equations to show the acid- and base-catalysed hydrolysis reactions of ethyl ethanoate. By using appropriate arrows between the two halves of each equation, show which is reversible and which is not.

1   Acid catalysed

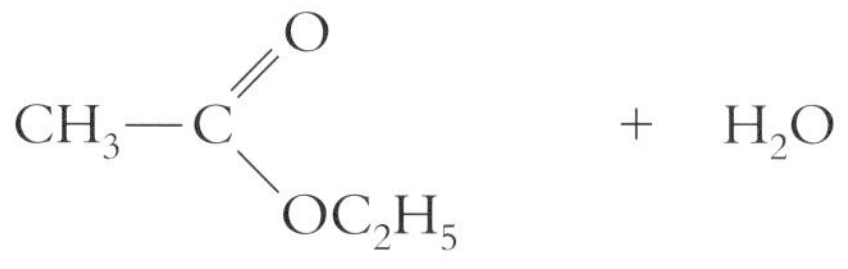

$$CH_3-C \overset{\displaystyle O}{\underset{\displaystyle OC_2H_5}{\diagdown}} \quad + \quad H_2O$$

2   Base catalysed

$$CH_3-C \overset{\displaystyle O}{\underset{\displaystyle OC_2H_5}{\diagdown}} \quad + \quad OH^-$$

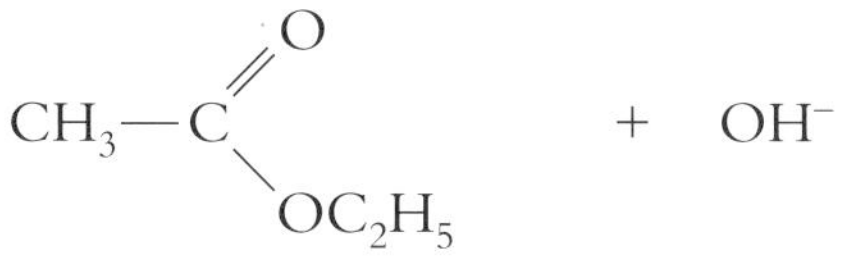

Ethene^{AS}

Complete this chart to show how ethene is converted to useful chemicals in industry.

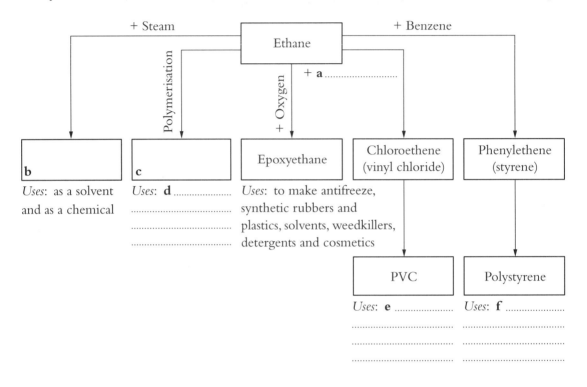

Uses: as a solvent
and as a chemical

Uses: **d** ....
....
....
....

Uses: to make antifreeze,
synthetic rubbers and
plastics, solvents, weedkillers,
detergents and cosmetics

Uses: **e** ....
....
....
....

Uses: **f** ....
....
....
....

Eutrophication^{AS}

Write down a sequence of numbers to arrange these sentences in order to make a paragraph describing eutrophication.

1 The nutrients from fertilisers make it possible for algae to multiply rapidly.	**2** As a result the plants cannot produce oxygen as fast as usual.	**3** Other organisms such as fish die because they are starved of oxygen.
4 Then bacteria start to break down the mass of algae using up oxygen in the water.	**5** Eutrophication happens when the water in rivers or lakes is enriched by fertilisers from farmland or by nutrients from sewage.	**6** Thick layers of algae block out the light from plants growing below the surface.

Fractional distillation of oil[AS]

Complete this diagram by suggesting uses for these fractions. Then answer the questions.

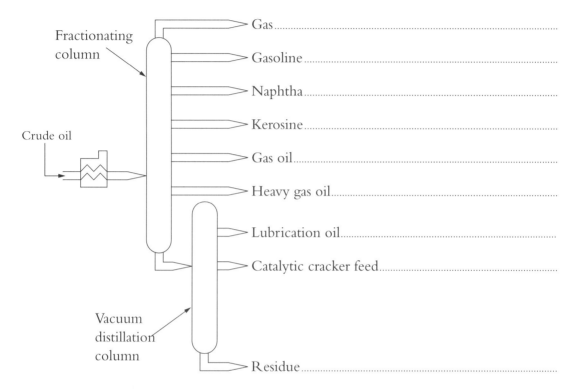

1 Give the structural formula and names of two refinery gases.

2 Draw the structure of a saturated hydrocarbon with the formula C_6H_{12}.

3 Explain why cracking is an important process in refining oil fractions. Give two reasons.

....

....

Free energy[A2]

Answer these questions about free energy, entropy and the feasibility of reactions.

1   What can you say about the sign of ΔG for a spontaneous reaction? ....

2   What is the relationship between ΔG, ΔH and ΔS for a reaction? ....

3   Why do chemists often choose to use the value of ΔH as an indicator of the spontaneity of reactions? ....

4   For the reaction:

$$2NO(g) + O_2(g) \rightarrow N_2O_4(g) \quad \Delta G^{\ominus} = -75.6 \text{ kJ mol}^{-1} \text{ at 298 K.}$$

Gas	$\Delta H_f^{\ominus}/\text{kJ mol}^{-1}$	$S^{\ominus}/\text{J mol}^{-1} \text{ K}^{-1}$
NO(g)	+ 90.2	210.7
O_2(g)	0	205.0
N_2O_4(g)	+ 9.2	304.2

Use the data provided to calculate, for this reaction:

a $\Delta H^{\ominus}$ ....

b $\Delta S^{\ominus}$ ....

c   The value of ΔG at 1000 K ....

d   Comment of the spontaneity of the reaction at:

         298 K ....

         1000 K ....

Free radical reaction[AS]

Complete this table to describe the three types of mechanistic step in the reaction of chlorine with methane.

Type of step	Description	Equation(s)
a	The step which produces free radicals	e
Propagation	c	f
b	d	$CH_3\bullet + CH_3\bullet \rightarrow CH_3CH_3$ $CH_3\bullet + Cl\bullet \rightarrow CH_3Cl$

Why does the reaction mixture include an excess of methane if the aim is to make chloromethane?

....

Friedel–Crafts reaction [A2]

Answer these questions about the Friedel–Crafts reaction.

1   Why is the Friedel–Crafts reaction important in both laboratory and industrial synthesis? ....

2   What is the usual catalyst for a Friedel–Crafts reaction and what is it about the electronic structure of the substance that makes it act as a catalyst for the process?

....

3   Complete this equation for a Friedel–Crafts reaction.

$$\bigcirc \quad + \quad CH_3CHCH_3 \quad \xrightarrow{\text{Catalyst}}$$
$$\underset{\displaystyle Cl}{|}$$

Fuels^AS

The maze contains the answers to these questions about fuels. The words are not in the same order as the questions. Move up or down, to the right or to the left but not diagonally to track the answers. Start in the top left corner.

1   A refinery process that turns cyclic alkanes into aromatic hydrocarbons such as benzene, which can be added to fuels for motor vehicles.

2   A type of fuel made from vegetable matter or organic wastes.

3   A blended fuel made from the gasoline fraction from oil refining.

4   A fuel made by fermentation of sugar.

5   The type of organic compound that makes up most of fuels made from crude oil.

R	P	E	O	L	K	I	N	G	O
E	G	T	R	F	C	N	E	N	C
F	N	S	S	O	A	U	M	A	T
O	I	I	L	C	R	E	B	S	O
R	M	N	I	K	C	R	G	A	H
E	D	G	E	N	O	N	K	L	O
N	Y	G	R	E	H	A	N	O	L
S	I	T	Y	E	T	I	B	L	D
C	O	R	D	Y	H	O	F	E	I
A	R	B	O	N	L	E	U	S	E

6   The fuel for motor vehicles that is responsible for causing most particulate pollution.

7   A blend of gasoline and ethanol which has been used as motor fuel in some countries such as Brazil.

8   The measure of the energy released per kilogram of fuel burnt (two words).

9   The scale used to measure the performance of fuel in motor engines (two words).

10   A process for turning high boiling compounds from the fractional distillation of oil into compounds suitable for making motor fuel.

11   A sound which a motorist may hear if the quality of the fuel is not good enough for the engine.

12   Coal, gas and oil are examples of this type of fuel.

Functional groups[AS]

Match the name of the homologous series with the example of a molecule with the functional group by drawing a line between the two. Also name the examples given.

1 primary alcohol

2 aldehyde

3 alkene

4 bromoalkane

5 carboxylic acid

6 chloroalkane

7 iodoalkane

8 ketone

9 secondary alcohol

10 tertiary alcohol

A

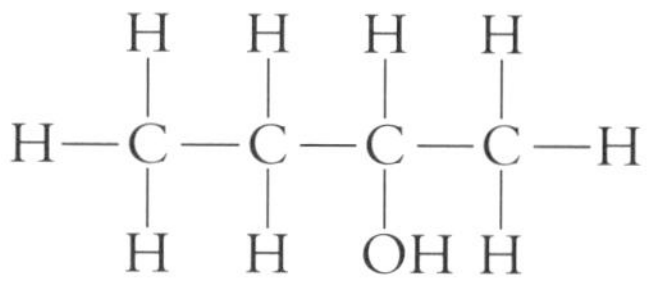

B

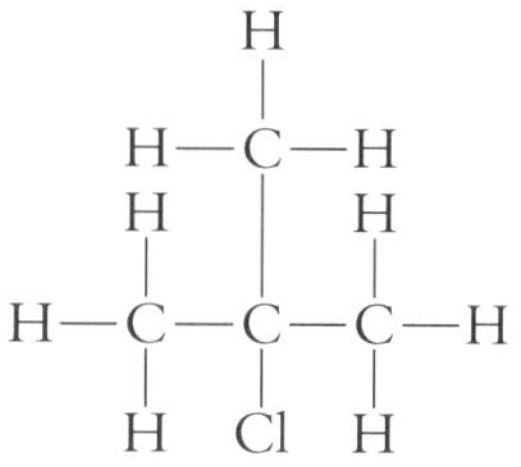

C

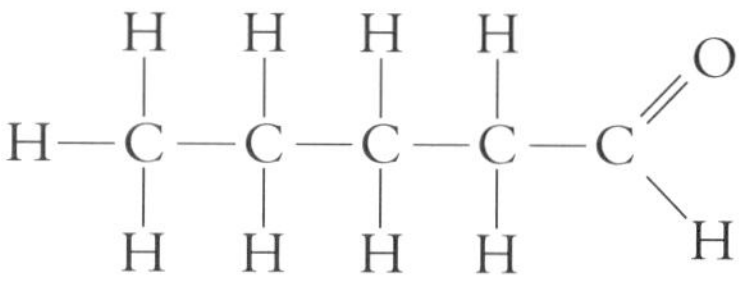

D

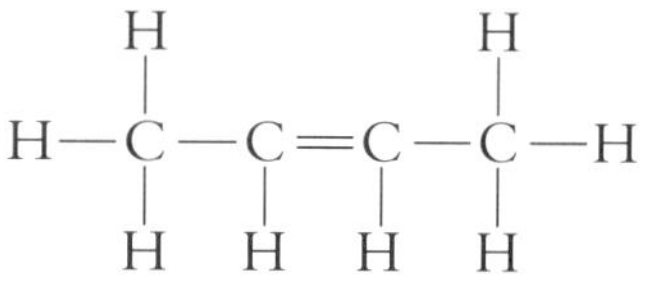

F

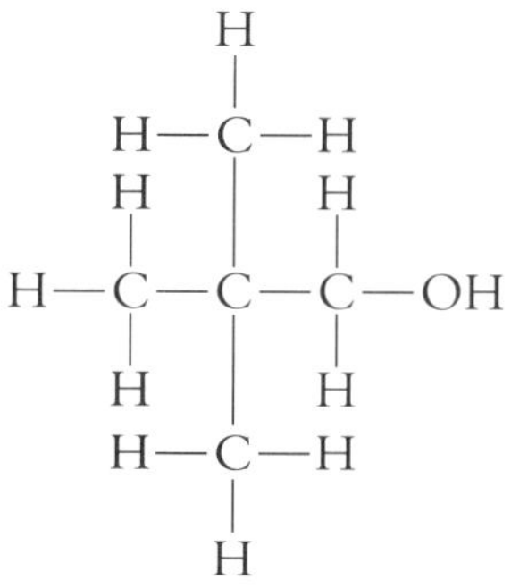

E

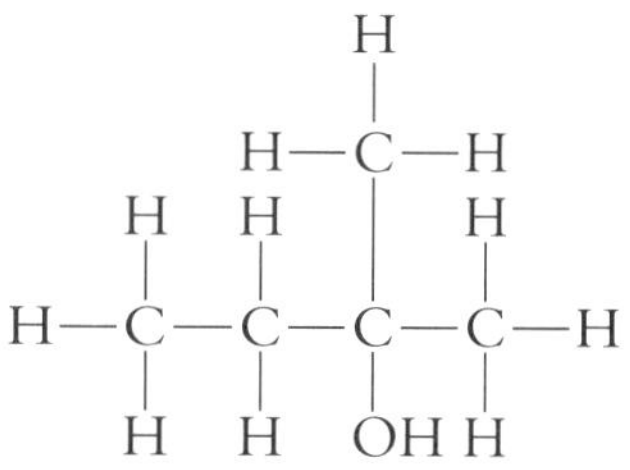

H

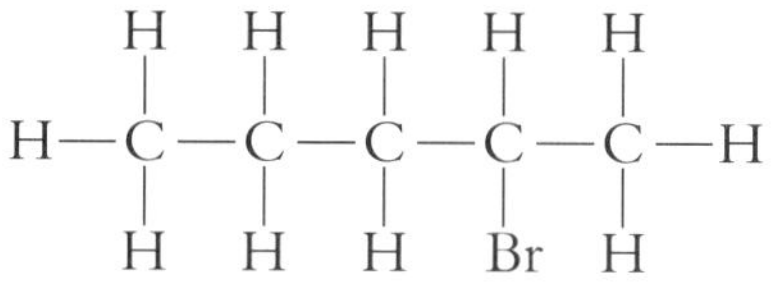

G

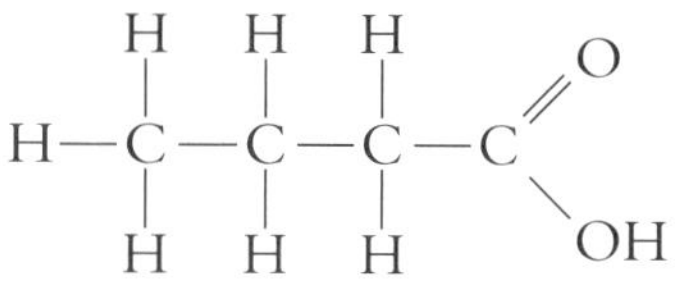

J

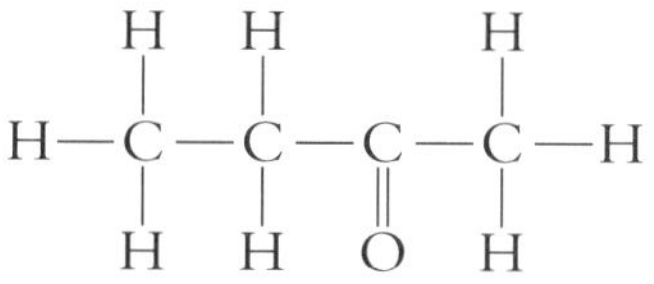

I

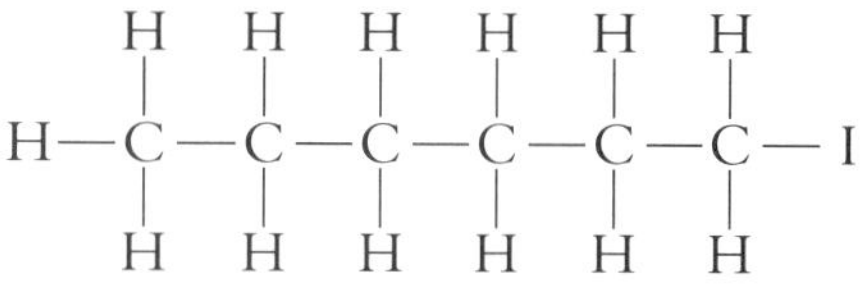

Functional groups^A2

Match the name of the homologous series with the example of a molecule with the functional group by drawing a line between the two. Also, name the examples given.

A $CH_3CH_2-C\underset{NH_2}{\overset{O}{\lessgtr}}$

B NO_2 (benzene ring)

C $CH_3C\underset{Cl}{\overset{O}{\lessgtr}}$

D CH_3 (benzene ring)

1   acid anhydride

2   acyl chloride

3   amide

4   amino acid

5   arene

6   ester

7   nitrile

8   nitroarene

9   phenol

10   primary alkyl amine

11   primary aryl (aromatic) amine

E NH_2 (benzene ring)

F $CH_3CH_2C\equiv N$

G $CH_3-C\overset{O}{\lessgtr}O$ $CH_3-C\underset{O}{\lessgtr}$

H $H_2N-\underset{H}{\overset{CH_3}{C}}-CO_2H$

I $CH_3CH_2NH_2$

J $CH_3CH_2C\underset{OCH_2CH_3}{\overset{O}{\lessgtr}}$

K OH (benzene ring)

Fundamental particles^AS

Complete the table alongside this diagram

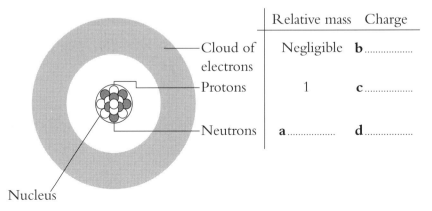

	Relative mass	Charge
Cloud of electrons	Negligible	**b** ....
Protons	1	**c** ....
Neutrons	**a**	**d** ....

Nucleus

Gas tests^{AS}

Identify the gas or gases given off in each of the reactions described.

1   Adding calcium metal to water produces a colourless gas that burns with a pop.

    ....

2   Heating magnesium nitrate produces an orange–brown mixture of gases that turns moist blue litmus paper red and relights a glowing splint. ....

3   Heating potassium nitrate strongly produces a colourless gas that relights a glowing splint. ....

4   Adding concentrated sulfuric acid to sodium chloride produces a colourless fuming gas that turns moist blue litmus paper red and gives a white smoke with ammonia gas. ....

5   Adding dilute nitric acid to magnesium carbonate produces a dense colourless gas that turns an aqueous solution of calcium hydroxide milky. ....

6   Warming potassium nitrate with aluminium foil produces a pungent gas that turns moist red litmus paper blue. ....

7   Adding concentrated hydrochloric acid to a solution of sodium chlorate(I) produces a greenish gas that bleaches moist litmus paper and turns starch–iodide paper blue black. ....

8   Warming dilute hydrochloric acid with sodium sulfite produces a colourless, pungent gas that turns moist blue litmus paper red and turns filter paper soaked in potassium dichromate(VI) from orange to green. ....

9   Heating crystals of calcium chloride produces a colourless, steamy vapour that turns cobalt(II) chloride paper from blue to pink. ....

10 Adding dilute hydrochloric acid to sodium sulfide produces a foul smelling gas that gives a brown–black colour with filter paper soaked with lead(II) ethanoate solution.

    ....

Gas volume calculations[AS]

Complete these two definitions.

- Avogadro's law states that .... volumes of gases under the same conditions of temperature and pressure contain .... numbers of molecules.

- The molar volume of a gas is the volume of .... of the gas under given conditions of .... and ....

Answer these questions that refer to reactions which involve only gases.

1   When 90 cm^3 hydrogen bromide reacts with 70 cm^3 ammonia a white solid forms and there is an excess of one gas. Which gas is in excess and what volume of this gas remains unchanged?

    ....

2   10 cm^3 of a hydrocarbon gas reacts with 90 cm^3 of oxygen to form 60 cm^3 of carbon dioxide with a little water. All volumes are measured under the same conditions. What is the formula of the hydrocarbon? ....

In the next question use the fact that, under normal laboratory conditions, the volume of one mole of gas is 24 dm^3 = 24 000 cm^3.

3   What volume of hydrogen, measured under normal laboratory conditions, is required to reduce 5.0 g Pb_3O_4 to metallic lead?

    ....

Geometric isomerism[AS]

Draw and name the structures of the two geometric isomers of an alkene with four carbon atoms.

Giant structures[AS]

These three diagrams represent very small fragments of crystal giant structures. State the type of bonding in each structure and give an example of a material with this type of structure.

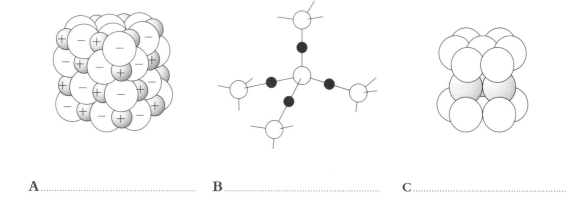

A .... B .... C ....

Grignard reagents[A2]

Complete this reaction scheme to illustrate the use of a Grignard reagent in synthesis. Name and classify the three products.

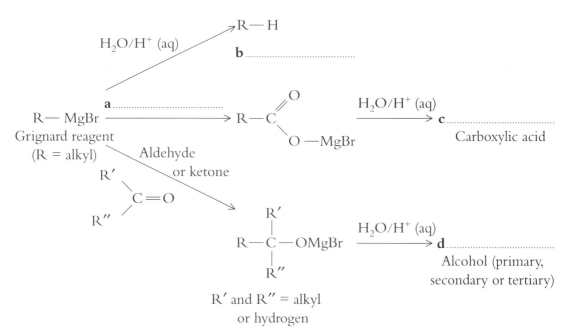

Group 1AS

Decide whether each of these statements about group 1 metals is true (T) or false (F). The symbol M stands for any group 1 metal.

1   The outer electron configuration of group 1 metal atoms is s^1. ....

2   When they react with non-metals the elements form 1+ ions. ....

3   The elements form ions that are larger than their atoms. ....

4   Any aqueous solution containing group 1 metal ions is alkaline. ....

5   The metals react with water to form hydrogen and the hydroxide MOH. ....

6   The flame colours produced by the salts of group 1 metals are either red or purple. ....

7   The metals are powerful reducing agents. ....

8   All the metals react with oxygen on heating to form one ionic oxide, M$_2$O. ....

9   The oxides of group 1 metals are basic. ....

10   The metals react with chlorine to form ionic, crystalline chlorides, MCl. ....

11   None of the group 1 metal carbonates decompose on heating in a Bunsen flame. ....

12   The group 1 metal carbonates are all insoluble in water. ....

13   The group 1 metal nitrates all decompose on heating to the nitrite and oxygen. ....

14   A white precipitate forms on adding sodium hydroxide solution to aqueous caesium chloride. ....

15   Solutions of the nitrates of group 1 metals are neutral. ....

Group 2AS

Write balanced equations for these reactions, including state symbols:

1   Magnesium with oxygen: ....

2   Magnesium with chlorine: ....

3   Magnesium with steam: ....

4   Calcium with water: ....

5   Barium oxide and dilute nitric acid: ....

6   Calcium hydroxide with dilute hydrochloric acid: ....

7   The thermal decomposition of magnesium carbonate: ....

8   The reaction on mixing aqueous solutions of barium nitrate and
    sodium sulfate: ....

Show whether the trend is for the following to increase or decrease down group 2.

A   The ionic radius ....

B   The first ionisation enthalpy ....

C   Rate of reaction of the metals with air and water ....

D   The thermal stability of the carbonates ....

E   The solubility in water of the hydroxides ....

F   The solubility in water of the sulfates ....

Group 4^{A2}

The answers to all these questions about group 4 are numbers.

1   The number of s-electrons in the outer shell of a group 4 element. **a** = ...

2   The number of p-electrons in the outer shell of a group 4 element. **b** = ...

3   The number of covalent bonds formed by a carbon atom in the diamond structure. **c** = ...

4   The number of sigma bonds formed by a carbon atom in the graphite structure. **d** = ...

5   The number of carbon atoms in the most familiar example of a buckyball. **e** = ...

6   The oxidation state of carbon in its neutral oxide. **f** = ...

7   The oxidation states of carbon and silicon in their acidic oxides. **g** = ...

8   The oxidation state in which tin and lead from their more basic oxides. **h** = ...

9   The oxidation state of the group 4 elements in their molecular chlorides. **i** = ...

10 The oxidation state which becomes less stable down the group.
    j = ...

11 The oxidation state which becomes more stable down the group.
    k = ...

12 The oxidation state of tin giving rise to compounds which are reducing agents. **l** = ...

Use your answers to work out the following.

The atomic number of germanium ($\mathbf{b} \times \mathbf{f} \times \mathbf{j} \times \mathbf{l}$) = ...

The hardness of diamond on Mohs' scale ($\mathbf{a} + \mathbf{c} + \mathbf{g}$) = ...

The approximate percentage of tin in bronze $4(\mathbf{k}^2 + 1)$ = ...

The melting point of silicon/°C $[(\mathbf{e}^2 \div 3) + 10\mathbf{d}(\mathbf{d} + \mathbf{i})]$ = ...

The transition temperature between grey tin and white tin/°C $[7\mathbf{f} - (\mathbf{h}^3 \div 10)]$ = ...

Halides^AS

Complete these four statements that describe similarities between three of the hydrogen halides HCl, HBr and HI.

Hydrogen chloride, hydrogen bromide and hydrogen iodide are similar in that they are all:

- .... gases at room temperature which .... in moist air,
- .... in water forming .... solutions (hydrochloric, hydrobromic and hydriodic acids),
- .... acids so they .... completely in water.

Complete the oxidation state diagram for the sulfur compounds mentioned in the three statements about the reactions of halides with concentrated sulfuric acid. Hence arrange the halide ions in order of their strengths as reducing agents.

- Chloride ions react with concentrated sulfuric acid to give hydrogen chloride as the only gaseous product.
- Bromide ions turn to orange bromine molecules as they reduce H_2SO_4 to SO_2, mixed with some hydrogen bromide gas,
- Iodide ions turn into iodine molecules as they reduce H_2SO_4 to S and H_2S, scarcely any hydrogen iodide forms.

.... > .... > ....

Complete this table to summarise the properties of silver halides and shows why they can be used to identify halide ions in solution.

Silver halide	Colour	Effect of adding ammonia solution to a precipitate of the compound
Silver chloride, AgCl	**a**..................	Dissolves **b**..................in ammonia solution
Silver bromide, **c**..................	cream	Dissolves but only in **d**.................. ammonia
e.................. AgI	yellow	Does **f**.................. dissolve even in concentrated ammonia solution

Halogenoalkanes[AS]

Complete this chart to summarise some of the reactions of 2-bromopropane. When the chart is complete, each box should contain the name and formula for a compound while each arrow is annotated with the reagents and conditions for the reaction.

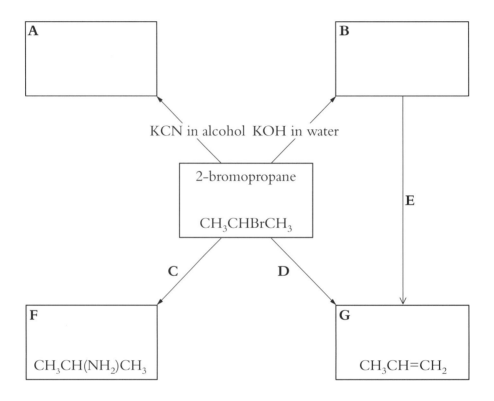

A

B

KCN in alcohol   KOH in water

2-bromopropane

$CH_3CHBrCH_3$

E

C   **D**

F

$CH_3CH(NH_2)CH_3$

G

$CH_3CH=CH_2$

Explain why halogenoalkanes are useful organic chemicals in the laboratory.

....

....

Halogens^AS

Write the answers to A–H into the grid. Then transfer letters from the numbered squares of the grid to the squares below with the same numbers to show up uses of four of these elements.

A The element with the electron configuration: $1s^2 2s^2 2p^6 3s^2 3p^5$

B The highly radioactive element in this family

A	1	2	3	4	5	6	7	8

B	9	10	11	12	13	14	15	16

C	17	18	19	20	21	22	23	24

D	25	26	27	28	29	30

E	31	32	33	34	35	36	37	38	39	40

F	41	42	43	44	45	46	47

G	48	49	50	51	52	53	54

H	55	56	57	58	59	60	61	62	63	64

C The most electronegative element

D The element which sublimes on heating turning from a shiny grey solid to a violet vapour

E The column of elements in the Periodic Table to which all these elements belong

F The general name for salts produced when these elements react with metals such as KI, AgBr, $MgCl_2$, AlF_3

G The element that oxidises iodide ions but not chloride ions

H What the name 'halo-gen' means – as illustrated by the reaction of chlorine with sodium

Examples of substances made from the elements or uses of the elements

Fluorine

35	58	17	8

Chlorine

48	18	37	12	1	41	6	53	31

Bromine

35	2	50	11	60	31	5	56	35	41	55

Iodine

35	41	9	64	51	42	1	39	34	13	25	1	42	57	36

Hess's law[AS]

Write down a relationship connecting the four enthalpy changes in the diagram, which follows from Hess's law.

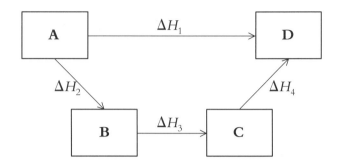

Write down a statement of Hess's law in words.

....

....

Heterogeneous catalysis[A2]

Beside the name of each heterogeneous catalysts write the letters of any of the chemical changes listed for which it is used as a catalyst. Also indicate the importance of each process.

Catalyst		*Reaction or process*	*Importance of the reaction*
Iron	**A**	Hydrogenation of unsaturated fatty acids in triglycerides	....
Nickel	**B**	Reaction of nitrogen with hydrogen to form ammonia	....
Platinum/ rhodium	**C**	Reaction of sulfur dioxide with oxygen to make sulfur trioxide	....
Silver	**D**	Reaction of ethene with oxygen to make epoxyethane	....
Vanadium(v) oxide	**E**	Oxidation of ammonia to nitrogen monoxide gas	....
Zeolite	**F**	Breakdown of hydrocarbons to smaller molecules	....
	G	Conversion of oxides of nitrogen to nitrogen and oxygen	....

Heterogeneous equilibrium[A2]

Answer these questions about an heterogeneous equilibrium.

1   Write the equation for the thermal decomposition of calcium carbonate.

....

2   Under what conditions can the reaction reach equilibrium?

....

3   Write an expression for K_c for this reaction.

....

4   Write an expression for K_p for this reaction.

....

Homogeneous catalysis[A2]

Fill the blanks in the sentence below, then match the catalysts with the reactions which they catalyse. Draw lines to link the items that match.

A homogeneous catalyst acts in the same .... as the reactants. Typically the reactants and the .... are dissolved in the same ....

Catalyst	Reaction
$Fe^{3+}(aq)$	**A** $2MnO_4^-(aq) + 5C_2O_4^{2-}(aq) + 16H^+(aq)$ $\rightarrow 2Mn^{2+}(aq) + 10CO_2(g) + 8H_2O(l)$
$H^+(aq)$	**B** $S_2O_8^{2-}(aq) + 2I^-(aq) \rightarrow 2SO_4^{2-}(aq) + I_2(aq)$
$Mn^{2+}(aq)$	**C** $C_4H_9CN(l) + 2H_2O(l) \rightarrow C_4H_9CO_2H(aq) + NH_3(aq)$

Homogeneous equilibrium[A2]

Answer these questions about an heterogeneous equilibrium.

1   Write the equation for the reversible hydrolysis of ethyl ethanoate in acid solution.

....

2   Under what conditions can the reaction reach equilibrium?

....

3   Write the expression for K_c for this reaction.

....

Ideal and real gases[AS]

Give the SI units for each of the quantities in the ideal gas equation.

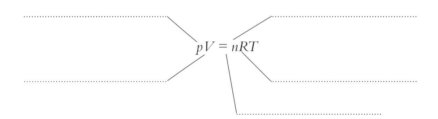

$$pV = nRT$$

Write the names of these gases in the appropriate column in this table: ammonia, argon, carbon dioxide, chlorine, helium, hydrogen, nitrogen, oxygen.

Behaviour is close to that of an ideal gas at room temperature and pressure	Behaviour at room temperature and pressure shows significant deviations from ideal behaviour

Infrared spectroscopy[A2]

Use the correlation chart to match the spectra with the named compounds.

Bond	*Characteristic wavenumber/cm^{-1}*
O—H not hydrogen bonded	3580–3670
O—H hydrogen bonded in alcohols and phenols	3550–3230
C—H aromatic	3150–3000
C—H aliphatic	3000–2850
O—H hydrogen bonded in carboxylic acids	2500–3300
C=O aldehydes, ketones, acids and esters	1750–1680
C—O alcohols, ethers and esters	1300–1000

A Butanal **B** Cyclohexane **C** Butan-1-ol **D** Ethyl ethanoate

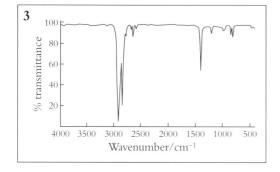

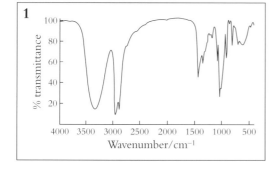

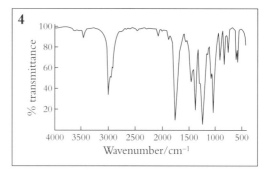

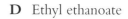

Initial rate method[A2]

The initial rate of reaction between nitrogen monoxide and hydrogen was measured in a series of experiments at 750 °C. The results showed that the rate equation is:

$$\text{rate} = k[H_2(g)][NO(g)]^2$$

Complete this table of data.

Experiment	Initial [$H_2(g)$]/ mol dm^{-3}	Initial [$NO(g)$]/ mol dm^{-3}	Initial rate mol dm^{-3} s^{-1}
1	0.001	0.006	0.00288
2	0.002	0.006	**a**
3	**b**	0.006	0.00862
4	0.006	0.001	0.00048
5	0.006	0.002	**c**
6	0.006	**d**	0.00432

Calculate a value for the rate contant k and give the units. ....

Intermediate bonding[AS]

Write in the formulae for these elements and compounds underneath the appropriate category in this spectrum of bonding: Br_2, HBr, $AlCl_3$, KF, O_2, BaO, MgI_2.

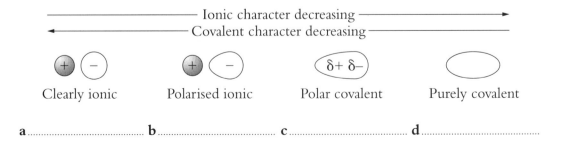

a................................ b............................... c............................... d................................

Intermediates in reactions[A2]

Identify the intermediate species formed during these reactions.

1   Reaction of chlorine with methane in UV light ....

2   Addition of hydrogen bromide to ethene ....

3   S_N1 substitution in 2-bromo-2-methylpropane ....

4   Electrophilic substitution of benzene with bromine ....

Intermolecular forces[AS]

Write the formulae of these molecular elements and compounds into the column of this table corresponding to the main forces between the molecules: NH_3, HBr, CH_4, Cl_2, H_2O, HF, CH_3Cl, C_2H_5OH, C_3H_8, $HCHO$.

Temporary dipole – temporary dipole	Permanent dipole – permanent dipole	Hydrogen bonding

Ionic bonding^AS

Complete these dot-and-cross diagrams to show the outer electron arrangements of the ions in three ionic compounds.

K   F   Mg   O   Cl   Ca   Cl

Complete this table to show how the properties of ionic crystals can be explained in terms of structure and bonding.

Property	Explanation
High melting and boiling points	**a**
b	Charged ions can move when the compound is molten but not when solid
c	Polar water molecules can hydrate ions. The hydration energies of the ions can be larger in magnitude than the lattice energy of the crystal
Brittle crystals which shatter if crushed	**d**

Ionic product of water[A2]

1   Write an equation to show the ionisation of pure water.

   ....

2   Write an expression for K_w. ....

3   In pure water what are the values of $[H^+(aq)]$ and $[OH^-(aq)]$? ....

4   What is the value of K_w? ....

Ionic radius[AS]

Write the symbols Na, Mg, Na$^+$ and Mg^{2+} in the appropriate circles to show the relative sizes of the atoms and ions of sodium and magnesium.

Write the symbols F, O, F$^-$ and O^{2-} in the appropriate circles to show the relative sizes of the atoms and ions of fluorine and chlorine.

What increases, what stays the same and what decreases along the series:

   N^{3-}, O^{2-}, F^-, Na^+, Mg^{2+}

   Increases: ....

   Stays the same: ....

   Decreases: ....

Ionisation enthalpy^AS

The sequences of numbers in the table below are the first six ionisation enthalpies of the elements: aluminium, calcium, potassium and silicon (but not in this order). Write the correct name of the elements in the matching box in the table.

Element	First six ionisation enthalpies in kilojoules per mole
a	419, 3051, 4412, 5877, 7975, 9649
b	789, 1577, 3232, 4356, 16 091, 19 785
c	590, 1145, 4912, 6474, 8144, 10 496
d	578, 1817, 2745, 11 578, 14 831, 18 378

The graph is a plot of log(ionisation enthalpy) against number of electrons removed for an element. Study the graph and answer the questions.

1   How many electrons are there in the outer shell of the element? ....

2   How many electrons are there in the innermost shell? ....

3   Name the element: ....

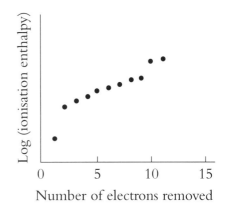

Label these two diagrams and add notes to explain why the first ionisation enthalpy for potassium is lower than the first ionisation enthalpy for sodium.

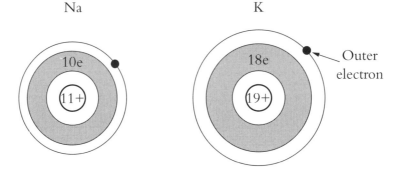

Na   K

Iron extraction[AS]

Label this diagram of a blast furnace to show: charge of ore, coke and limestone; blast of hot air, molten iron, molten slag and tap hole. Then write equations for the chemical reactions in the blast furnace which heat the furnace, create the reducing agent, reduce the ore to metal and convert sandy impurities to slag.

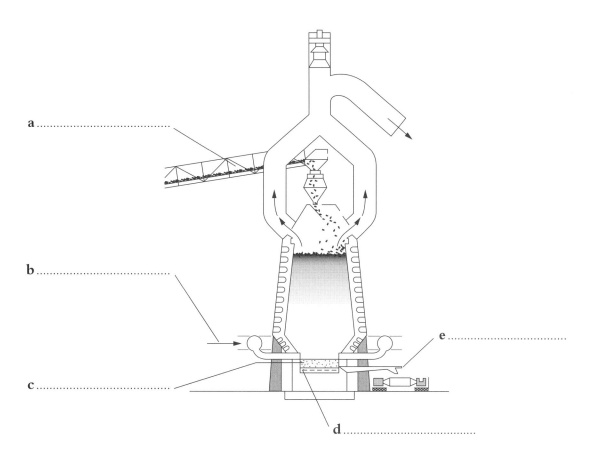

a ....

b ....

c ....

d ....

e ....

Equations for reactions

....

....

....

....

Isomerism[A2]

Complete this chart by adding examples to the boxes to summarise the types of isomerism in organic chemistry.

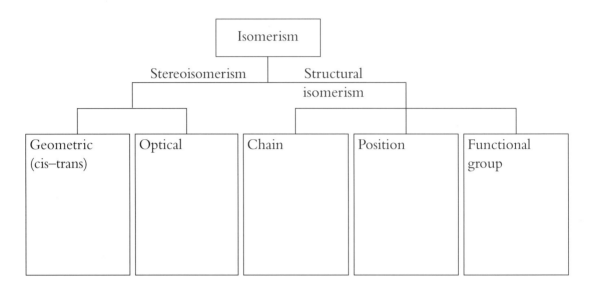

Isotopes[AS]

Complete this table which shows the isotopes of several elements.

Isotope	Protons	Neutrons	Electrons
$^{2}_{1}H$	1	a	b
$^{3}_{1}H$	c	2	d
$^{12}_{6}C$	6	6	6
$^{14}_{6}C$	e	f	g
$^{88}_{38}Sr$	h	50	i
$^{90}_{38}Sr$	j	k	l

K_a A2

Answer these questions with the help of the data provided.

Acid	K_a/mol dm^{-3}
Methanoic acid, HCO_2H	1.6×10^{-4}
Ethanoic acid, CH_3CO_2H	1.7×10^{-5}
Phenol, C_6H_5OH	1.3×10^{-10}

1 Write an equation for the ionisation of methanoic acid. ....

2 Write the expression for K_a for methanoic acid.

3 Why does the term $[H_2O(l)]$ not appear in the expression for K_a? ....

4 Which is the weakest acid in the table? ....

5 Justify the two approximations that can simplify the calculation of the hydrogen ion concentration and pH of a solution of a weak acid, HA.

Assumption 1: $[H_3O^+(aq)] = [A^-(aq)]$.
(For methanoic acid, A^- is the methanoate ion.)

Justification: ....

Assumption 2: That so little of the weak acid ionises in water that:
$[HA(aq)]_{equilibrium} \approx [HA(aq)]_{initial}$

where HA represents the unionised acid.

Justification: ....

6 Calculate the pH of a 0.01 mol dm^{-3} solution of methanoic acid.

pH = ...

$$K_c \text{ A2}$$

Answer these questions.

1   Write the expression for K_c for each of these equilibria. In each case give the units of K_c if any.

   a $H_2(g) + I_2(g) \rightleftharpoons 2HI(g)$

   b $PCl_5(g) \rightleftharpoons PCl_3(g) + Cl_2(g)$

2   When a sample of PCl_5 reaches equilibrium with PCl_3 and chlorine at 250 °C in a 2 dm^3 container the amounts of substances present are: $PCl_5(g) = 0.036$ mol, $PCl_3(g) = 0.15$ mol, and $Cl_2 = 0.090$ mol. Calculate the value of K_c under these conditions.

....

3   For an equilibrium mixture formed by the reaction of $H_2(g)$ with $I_2(g)$ at 450 °C $K_c = 61$. Calculate the amount of hydrogen iodide at equilibrium when 20.57 mol hydrogen and 5.22 mol I_2 are mixed and kept at 450 °C.

....

$$K_p \text{ A2}$$

Write the expression for K_p for each of these equilibria. In each case give the units if any.

Equilibrium	K_p	Units of K_p (using the SI unit of pressure, Pa)
$H_2(g) + I_2(g) \rightleftharpoons 2HI(g)$	$K_p =$	
$N_2(g) + 3H_2(g) \rightleftharpoons 2NH_3(g)$	$K_p =$	
$N_2O_4(g) \rightleftharpoons 2NO_2(g)$	$K_p =$	

Ketones[A2]

Complete this table to show some of the reactions of propanone.

Reactant	Reagent	Type of reaction	Organic product	
			Name	Displayed formula
CH_3COCH_3	Fehling's solution	a	b	c
CH_3COCH_3	$NaBH_4$	d	e	f
CH_3COCH_3	g	h	2-hydroxy-2-methylpropane nitrile	i

Le Chatelier's principle[AS]

Use Le Chatelier's principle to answer these questions.

1   The reaction of ethene with steam in the presence of a phosphoric acid catalyst is used to manufacture ethanol. The reaction is exothermic.

Write the equation for the reaction: ....

Predict qualitatively the conditions needed for the maximum yield of ethanol and give reasons.

Pressure: ....

Temperature: ....

2   Synthesis gas is a mixture of carbon monoxide and hydrogen made from natural gas and steam. The reaction is endothermic.

Write the equation for the reaction: ....

Predict qualitatively the conditions needed for the maximum yield of products and give reasons.

Pressure: ....

Temperature: ....

3   Ethanoic acid ionises in solution:
$$CH_3CO_2H(aq) + H_2O(l) \rightleftharpoons CH_3CO_2^-(aq) + H_3O^+(aq)$$

What would be the effect in each case on adding the following to a fresh 100 cm^3 sample of 0.1 mol dm^{-3} ethanoic acid and then thoroughly stirring the mixture?

a 1 dm^3 water ....

b   20 g sodium ethanoate ....

c 10 cm^3 concentrated hydrochloric acid ....

d 100 cm^3 0.1 mol dm^{-3} sodium hydroxide ....

Lewis acids and bases[A2]

Label the Lewis acid and the Lewis base in each of these equations. Then give a definition of a Lewis acid and a Lewis base.

$$H^+ \ + \ :\overset{\displaystyle H}{\underset{..}{O}}-H \ \longrightarrow \ H-\overset{\displaystyle H}{\underset{..}{O}}-H \ ^+$$

$$Ni^{2+} \ + \ 6:NH_3 \ \longrightarrow \ [Ni(NH_3)_6]^{2+}$$

$$\underset{\displaystyle Cl}{\overset{\displaystyle Cl}{Cl-Al}} \ + \ Cl-Cl \ \longrightarrow \ \underset{\displaystyle Cl}{\overset{\displaystyle Cl}{Cl-Al-Cl}} \ ^- \ + \ Cl^+$$

A Lewis acid is ....

A Lewis base is ....

Ligands[A2]

Name these ligands. Classify them to show whether they are monodentate, bidentate or hexadentate.

$$\underset{\text{-}O}{\overset{O}{\underset{\diagdown}{\overset{\diagup}{C}}}}-\underset{O^-}{\overset{O}{\overset{\diagup}{\underset{\diagdown}{C}}}}$$

$$NH_3$$

$$\begin{array}{l} \diagup N(CH_2CO_2^-)_2 \\ CH_2 \\ | \\ CH_2 \\ \diagdown N(CH_2CO_2^-)_2 \end{array}$$

$$H_2O$$

$$H_2NCH_2CH_2NH_2$$

Markovnikov's rule[AS/A2]

Fill in the missing words.

Markovnikov's rule predicts the main product when a compound HX (such as H—Br, H—HSO_4 or H—OH) adds to an unsymmetrical .... (such as propene). The rule is that the .... atom adds to the carbon atom which already has .... hydrogen atoms attached to it.

Draw the structure of the main product of each of these changes. Name the organic product.

$$CH_3—CH{=}CH_2 \ + \ HBr \longrightarrow$$

$$CH_3—\underset{\underset{CH_3}{|}}{C}{=}CH_2 \ + \ H_2O \ \xrightarrow{\text{Catalyst}}$$

Label these carbocations as primary, secondary or tertiary and show the order of stability of the ions.

$$\underset{\underset{H}{|}}{\overset{CH_3}{\diagdown}}\overset{+}{C}\overset{H}{\diagup} \qquad \underset{\underset{H}{|}}{\overset{CH_3}{\diagdown}}\overset{+}{C}\overset{CH_3}{\diagup} \qquad \underset{\underset{CH_3}{|}}{\overset{CH_3}{\diagdown}}\overset{+}{C}\overset{CH_3}{\diagup}$$

Alkyl groups tend to release electrons towards neighbouring groups. This is an example of the .... effect. This effect can help to stabilise carbocations by '...........................' the charge over the ion.

The relative stability of .... and the mechanism for .... addition to alkenes helps to account for Markovnikov's rule. On adding HBr to propene there are two possible intermediate carbocations. The .... carbocation is preferred because it is slightly more .... than the primary carbocation.

Mass spectrometry^AS

Below is a simplified diagram of a mass spectrometer with several parts unnumbered. On the left is a list of descriptions. Match the numbers on the diagram with the letters of the descriptors.

A Ion detector ....

B Sample bombarded by electrons and turned into positive ions ....

C Heavier particles ....

D Signal from detector amplified and recorded ....

E Sample injected into the instrument where it vaporises ....

F Lighter particles ....

G Electric field to accelerate the positive ions ....

H Beam of particles focussed on the detector ....

Lead has four isotopes with these abundances: lead-204 (1.5%), lead-206 (23.6%), lead 207 (22.6%) and lead-208 (52.3%).

Calculate the mean relative atomic mass of lead by completing the gaps below and working out the result. What are the units, if any, of relative atomic mass?

The average relative atomic mass of lead

$$= \frac{(\quad \times \quad) + (\quad \times \quad) + (\quad \times \quad) + (\quad \times \quad)}{100}$$

$$= \ ....$$

Mass spectrometry^A2

Examine the mass spectrum of ethanol. Match the numbered peaks with the formulae for the positive ions which are formed from ethanol molecules at low pressure in a mass spectrometer. Then answer the questions.

A $C_2H_5^+$ ....

B CH_2OH^+ ....

C $C_2H_5O^+$ ....

D $C_2H_5OH^+$ ....

E $C_2H_3^+$ ....

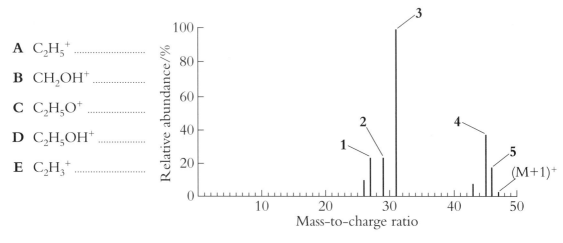

1   Write an equation to show the formation of the molecular ion?

    ....

2   **a**   Write an equation show how the molecular ion fragments to give fragment B.

    ....

    b   What other species is formed during this fragmentation process and why does it not show up in the mass spectrum?

    ....

3   **a**   Why is there a peak labelled (M + 1)?

    ....

    b   What can be deduced from the fact that in this mass spectrum the (M + 1) peak is about 2.2% of the height of the molecular ion peak?

    ....

Maxwell–Boltzmann distribution[AS]

Label the axes of this graph, which shows the Maxwell–Boltzmann distribution of molecular energies in a gas at two temperatures. Then annotate the graph with these phrases: distribution of molecular energies at a lower temperature, distribution of molecular energies at a higher temperature, activation energy. Shade two areas: one to show the proportion of molecules able to react at the lower temperature and the other to show the proportion of molecules able to react at a higher temperature.

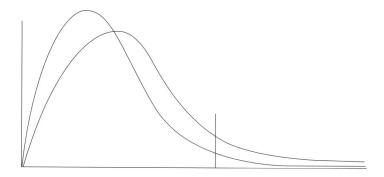

Write two or three sentences to explain the effect of temperature on reaction rate based on the two graphs.

....

....

....

....

Metallic bonding^AS

Complete this table to show how the properties of metals can be explained in terms of structure and bonding.

Property	Explanation
High melting and boiling points	**b**
a	Atoms held together by the cloud of delocalised electrons so that the bonding is not directional
Good conductors of electricity	**c**
Insoluble in water and organic solvents	**d**

Molecular formula^AS

Fill in the blanks in this table.

Substance	Empirical formula	Relative molecular mass	Molecular formula
Ammonia	**a**	**b**	NH_3
Butane	C_2H_5	58	**c**
Hydrogen peroxide	**d**	34	**e**

Nitration of benzene[A2]

State the conditions for the nitration of benzene to introduce one nitro group. Complete this reaction scheme to show the formation of the electrophile for the reaction and name the electrophile.

Conditions: ....

$$HO\text{—}NO_2 + H_2SO_4 \longrightarrow HO^+\text{—}NO_2 + HSO_4^-$$
$$\phantom{HO\text{—}NO_2 + H_2SO_4 \longrightarrow HO^+}| $$
$$\phantom{HO\text{—}NO_2 + H_2SO_4 \longrightarrow HO^+}H$$

Complete this outline mechanism for the nitration reaction.

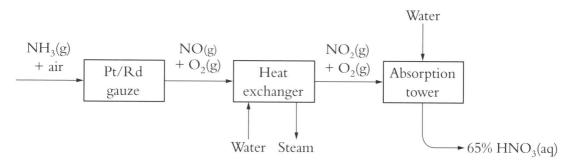

This is an example of e .... s ....

Give two reasons why the nitration of arenes is economically important.

....

Nitric acid manufacture[AS]

Write the equations for the three main reactions represented by this flow diagram for the manufacture of nitric acid.

Pt/Rd gauze: ....

```
                                                          Water
                                                            ↓
 NH₃(g)                    NO(g)                 NO₂(g)
 + air    ┌─────────┐     + O₂(g)   ┌─────────┐  + O₂(g)   ┌─────────────┐
 ───────→ │  Pt/Rd  │ ──────────→   │  Heat   │ ─────────→ │ Absorption  │
          │  gauze  │               │exchanger│            │   tower     │
          └─────────┘               └─────────┘            └─────────────┘
                                      ↑      ↓                    └──→ 65% HNO₃(aq)
                                   Water  Steam
```

Cooling: ....

Absorption: ....

Nitriles[A2]

Give the names and structures of the starting materials for two methods of making nitriles.

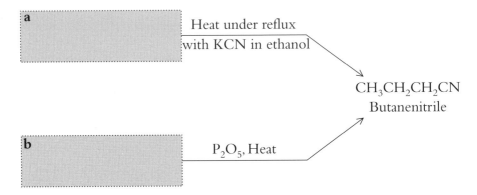

a [blank box]

Heat under reflux
with KCN in ethanol

$CH_3CH_2CH_2CN$
Butanenitrile

b [blank box]

P_2O_5, Heat

Give the names and structures of the products for these two reactions of nitriles.

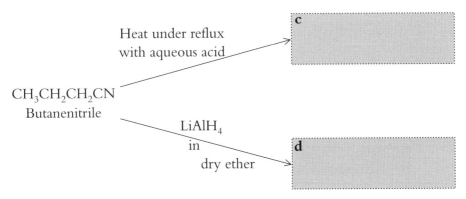

Heat under reflux
with aqueous acid

c [blank box]

$CH_3CH_2CH_2CN$
Butanenitrile

$LiAlH_4$
in
dry ether

d [blank box]

Complete this reaction scheme and explain its importance in synthesis.

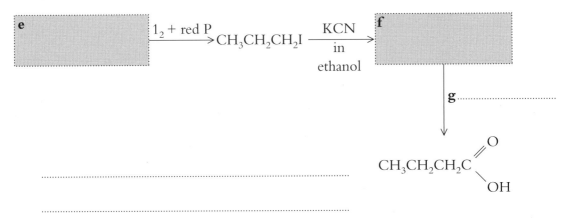

e [blank box]

I_2 + red P

$CH_3CH_2CH_2I$

KCN
in
ethanol

f [blank box]

g ·······························

$CH_3CH_2CH_2C\overset{\displaystyle O}{\underset{\displaystyle OH}{}}$

···

···

nmr spectroscopy

Match the low resolution nmr spectra with the four named compounds with the help of the table of chemical shifts.

Type of proton	Chemical shift/ppm
$R—CH_3$	0.9
$R—CH_2—R$	1.3
$R_3C—H$	2.0
$CH_3—CO_2R$	2.0
$CH_3—CO—R$	2.1
$R—CH_2—CO—R$	2.5
$R—O—CH_3$	3.8
$R—O—H$	3.5–5.5
$R—CHO$	9.7
$R—CO_2H$	11.0–11.7

A Cyclohexane **B** Hexane **C** Ethanoic acid **D** Butanone

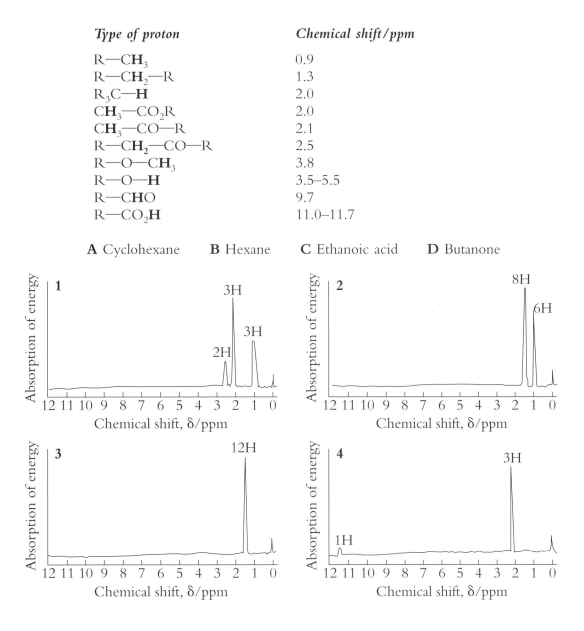

Nucleophilic addition^{AS/A2}

1   Identify two nucleophiles which react with aldehydes and ketones. ....

2   Why is the carbon atom of a carbonyl group open to nucleophilic attack?

     ....

3   Add curly arrows and show the structure of the product of the first step of
     nucleophilic addition of hydrogen cyanide.

$$N\equiv C^- \quad \begin{array}{c} CH_3 \\ \diagdown \\ C=O \\ \diagup \\ CH_3 \end{array} \quad \longrightarrow$$

4   Add curly arrows and show the structure of the product of the second step of
     nucleophilic addition of hydrogen cyanide.

$$N\equiv C-\overset{\overset{\displaystyle CH_3}{|}}{\underset{\underset{\displaystyle CH_3}{|}}{C}}-O^- \quad H-CN \quad \longrightarrow$$

Nucleophilic substitution^{AS/A2}

*Add curly arrows and complete these summaries for two mechanisms for nucleophilic
substitution in halogenoalkanes. Indicate the rate-determining step for each
mechanism and complete the rate equation associated with each mechanism. Identify
the S_N1 and S_N2 mechanisms.*

$$S_N\text{..........} \quad HO^- \quad \begin{array}{c} H \quad H \\ \diagdown \; \vdots \\ C-Br \\ \diagup \\ CH_3 \end{array} \quad \longrightarrow \qquad\qquad + Br^-$$

Rate =...

$$S_N\text{..........} \quad \begin{array}{c} CH_3 \quad CH_3 \\ \diagdown \; \vdots \\ C-Br \\ \diagup \\ CH_3 \end{array} \quad \longrightarrow \quad \begin{array}{c} CH_3 \diagdown \overset{+}{} \diagup CH_3 \\ C \\ | \\ CH_3 \end{array} \quad \overset{\displaystyle OH^-}{\longrightarrow}$$
$$+ \; Br^-$$

Rate =...

Optical isomerism^A2

Answer the questions and fill in the grid to reveal the term chemists use to describe a mixture of equal amounts of the two mirror image forms of a compound that shows optical isomerism.

1   A term to describe a compound that has optical isomers.

2   A term to describe the two optical isomers of a compound.

3   The traditional name for an acid with optical isomers found in sour milk and in muscles during anaerobic exercise.

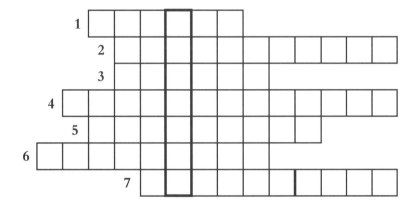

4   Distinct compounds with the same molecular formula and structural formulae but with different three-dimensional shapes.

5   A feature of organic molecules with four different groups or atoms bonded to a carbon atom.

6   The direction of rotation of this type of light distinguishes the optical isomers of a compound.

7   A description of the part of a protein responsible for its effectiveness as an enzyme that generally is effective with one optical isomer of a compound but not with its mirror image.

Orders of reaction[A2]

The graphs show concentration–time graphs and rate–concentration graphs for zero-, first- and second-order reactions. Identify which is which.

CONCENTRATION–TIME GRAPHS

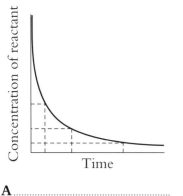

A ....

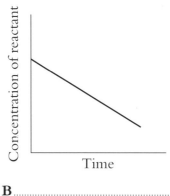

B ....

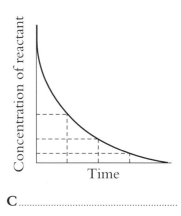

C ....

RATE–CONCENTRATION GRAPHS

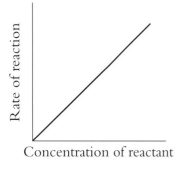

D ....

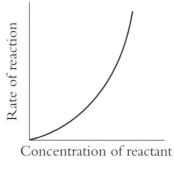

E ....

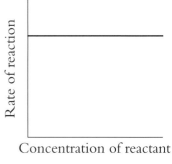

F ....

Organic preparations

Match the entries in the table with the stages in carrying out an organic preparation.

A Shaking immiscible reactants in a stoppered container	**B** Solvent extraction	**C** Fractional distillation
D Recrystallisation	**E** nmr spectroscopy	**F** Heating a mixture in a flask fitted with a reflux condenser
G Thin-layer chromatography	**H** Vacuum filtration	**I** Measuring melting points
J Steam distillation	**K** Infrared spectroscopy	**L** Distillation
M Adding chemical reagents to small samples in test tubes	**N** Measuring boiling points	**O** Leaving to stand with a little anhydrous sodium sulfate or calcium chloride

Carrying out the reaction ....

Separating the product from the reaction mixture ....

Purifying the product ....

Identifying the product and testing its purity ....

Organic synthesis[A2]

Identify the reagents and state the conditions for the stages of these syntheses.

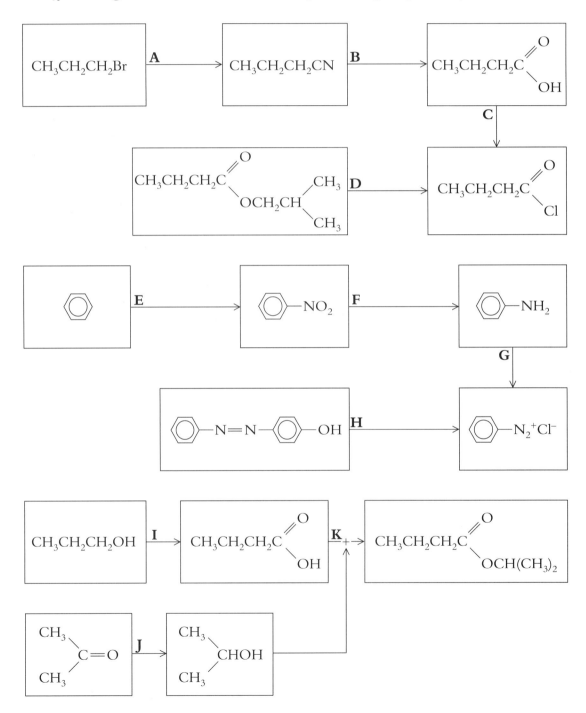

Oxidation numbers[AS]

Give the oxidation numbers of the named elements in these examples:

1 Oxygen in Al_2O_3 ....

2 Vanadium in V_2O_5 ....

3 Phosphorus in P_4O_{10} ....

4 Copper in $CuCl$ ....

5 Chlorine in $KClO_3$ ....

6 Copper in $Cu(NO_3)_2$ ....

7 Oxygen in H_2O_2 ....

8 Sulfur in H_2SO_3 ....

Are these elements oxidised or reduced in these conversions?

9 $I_2 \rightarrow I_2O_5$ ....

10 $Cl_2 \rightarrow PCl_5$ ....

11 $O_2 \rightarrow OF_2$ ....

12 $H_2 \rightarrow NaH$ ....

Use oxidation numbers to balance these equations for redox reactions.

13 .... $NaIO_3(aq)$ + ... $NaI(aq)$ + ... $H_2SO_4(aq) \rightarrow$

.... $I_2(aq)$ + ... $H_2O(l)$ + ... $Na_2SO_4(aq)$

14 .... $Cu(s)$ + ... $HNO_3(aq) \rightarrow$ .... $Cu(NO_3)_2(aq)$ + ... $NO_2(g)$ + ... $H_2O(l)$

15 .... $Cl_2(aq)$ + ... $NaOH(aq) \rightarrow$ .... $NaClO(aq)$ + ... $NaCl(aq)$ + ... $H_2O(l)$

16 .... $MnO_4^-(aq)$ + ... $H^+(aq)$ + ... $Fe^{2+}(aq) \rightarrow$.

.... $Mn^{2+}(aq)$ + ... $Fe^{3+}(aq)$ + ... $H_2O(l)$

Oxides[A2]

Classify the oxides of these elements as basic, amphoteric, acidic or neutral by writing the formulae of the oxides into the correct column in the table: aluminium, barium, beryllium, calcium, carbon, copper, lead, magnesium, nitrogen, phosphorus, sodium, sulfur, zinc. Include more than one oxide for an element where appropriate.

Basic	Amphoteric	Acidic	Neutral

Oxidising agents[AS]

GEORGE, NAOMI, PATRICIA, RHODA, SIMON, ALEX, YVONNE, PAT and RUPERT were revising chemistry and trying to recall the names of common oxidising agents. Use the letters of their names (once each) to reveal the names of the examples they came up with.

O _ Y _ _ _   _ O _ _ S _ _ U _ D I C _ _ _ _ _ T _ (VI)

B _ _ M _ _ E   _ _ _ _ SS _ _ M M _ _ G _ _ _ _ _ (_II)

_ H _ _ _ INE   H _ D _ O _ _ N _ _ _ _ X _ _ E

Partial pressures[A2]

Fill in the gaps in these sentences.

The total pressure of a mixture of gases is the .... of the partial pressures.

Each gas makes its own independent contribution to the ....

Partial pressures are a useful alternative to concentrations when studying .... involving gases. In a mixture of gases A, B and C the sum of the three partial pressures equals the total pressure: $p_{total} = p_A + $ .... $ + $ ....

The total pressure in a mixture can be 'shared out' between the gases according their mole fractions, X. So:

$$p_A = \text{...............}, \quad p_B = X_B p_{total}, \quad \text{and} \quad p_C = \text{...............}$$

Period 3 elements[A2]

Create a table below to summarise the structure and bonding of period 3 elements. Which are metals and which are non metals? Which have giant structures and which are molecular? In which is the strong bonding metallic and in which is it covalent? In which are the physical properties determined by weak intermolecular forces?

$$Na \quad Mg \quad Al \quad Si \quad P_{white} \quad O \quad S \quad Cl \quad Ar$$

Period 3 chlorides[A2]

Complete this table to summarise the chemistry of the chlorides of elements in period 3.

	Chloride of sodium	Chloride of magnesium	Chloride of aluminium	Chloride of silicon	Chloride of phosphorous
Formula					
State at room temperature and pressure					
Type of structure					
Type of bonding					
Extent of hydrolysis with water					

Summarise the behaviour of three of the chlorides in water.

Reaction of the chloride of aluminium with water:

Equation ....

Reaction of the chloride of silicon with water:

Equation ....

Reaction with water of the chloride of phosphorus that has the lower oxidation state:

Equation ....

Period 3 oxides[A2]

Complete this table to summarise the chemistry of three oxides of elements in period 3.

	Compound of magnesium with oxidation	Compound of silicon with oxygen	Compound of sulfur with oxygen
Formula			
State at room temperature and pressure			
Type of structure			
Type of bonding			
Type of oxide			

Summarise the behaviour of the three oxides in water.

Reaction of magnesium oxide with water:

Equation ....

Approximate pH of the solution: ....

Reaction of an oxide of sulfur with water:

Equation ....

Approximate pH of the solution: ....

Periodic table[AS]

Solve the clues and enter them in the grid to reveal a name used to describe many of the metals in the d-block of the Periodic table.

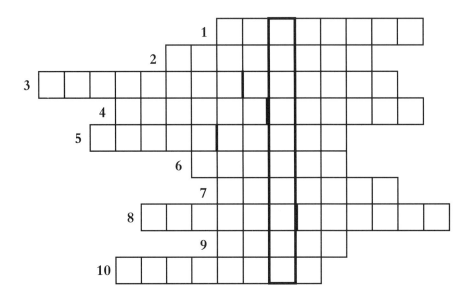

1   The element with the electron configuration $1s^2 2s^2 2p^3$.

2   The most electronegative element.

3   A common description of the group 2 metals.

4   The quantity which determines the order of elements in the periodic table.

5   A family of very unreactive elements.

6   A horizontal row in the Periodic Table.

7   The group 1 metal with the smallest atomic radius and the highest first ionisation enthalpy.

8   The family of s-block metals which form 1+ ions.

9   A vertical column of elements in the periodic table.

10 The family of 'salt forming' elements.

Periodicity of physical properties^{AS}

MELTING POINTS OF THE ELEMENTS

Write the symbols for the elements alongside the dots of this plot of melting point against atomic number for the elements Li to Ar.

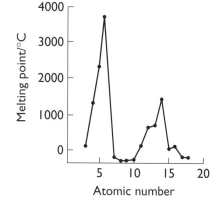

1   Which of the elements Li to Ar have giant structures? ....

2   Which of the elements Li to Ar have molecular structures? ....

3   In which of the elements Li to Ar is the bonding metallic? ....

4   In which of the elements Li to Ar is the strong bonding covalent? ....

5   Why is there a sharp drop in melting points between groups 4 and 5 in each period?

....

FIRST IONISATION ENTHALPIES

Write the symbols for the elements alongside the dots of this plot of first ionisation enthalpy against atomic number for the elements H to Ca.

6   Why do first ionisation enthalpies tend to increase across a period? ....

7   Why is the first ionisation enthalpy of boron lower than the value for beryllium? ....

8   Why is the first ionisation enthalpy of oxygen lower than the value for nitrogen? ....

9   Why do first ionisation enthalpies tend to decrease down a group? ....

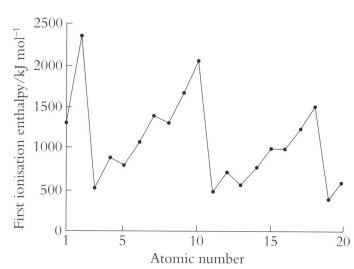

pH^{A2}

Pick a quantity from the left-hand column and combine it with a term from the right-hand column to form a relationship used in pH calculations. Write the relationship on the appropriate line below.

pH	$- \log K_a$
K_w	$[H^+(aq)][A^-(aq)]/[HA(aq)]$
K_a	$- \log [H^+(aq)]$
pK_a	10^{-pH}
$[H^+(aq)]$	$[H^+(aq)][OH^-(aq)]$

The definition of pH ....

The hydrogen ion concentration in a solution ....

The ionic product of water ....

The application of the equilibrium law to the ionisation of a weak acid, HA ....

....

A logarithmic form of the acid dissocation constant ....

State or work out the pH value of the following, then substitute the values in the expression given to find the year in which the Danish biochemist, Sören Sörensen, invented the pH scale.

a   The pH of a 0.01 mol dm^{-3} solution of hydrochloric acid ....

b   The pH of a 0.0001 mol dm^{-3} solution of sodium hydroxide ....

c   The pH of a 0.10 mol dm^{-3} solution of ethanoic acid ....
($K_a = 1.7 \times 10^{-5}$ mol dm^{-3}, pK_a = 3.8)

d   The pH of 0.1 mol dm^{-3} solution of nitric acid ....

Date = $[(\mathbf{c} - \mathbf{d}) \times \mathbf{b}^3] + (\mathbf{a} + \mathbf{d})^2$ = ...

pH changes during acid–base titrations[A2]

These graphs show the pH changes on adding a 0.1 mol dm^{-3} alkali to 25 cm^3 of a 0.1 mol dm^{-3} acid. Beside each graph indicate whether or not the acid and the base is strong or weak.

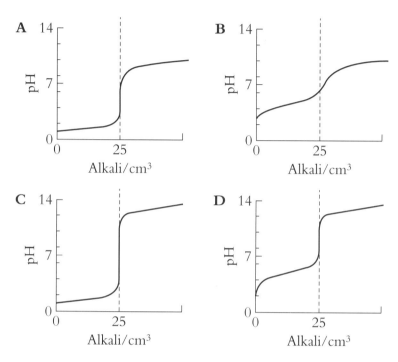

Choose, where possible, an appropriate indicator to detect the end-point for each titration. Mark on the corresponding graph the pH range over which your chosen indicator changes colour.

Indicator	pK_a	Colour change HIn/In$^-$	pH range over which colour change occurs
Methyl orange	3.7	Red/yellow	3.2–4.4
Methyl red	5.1	Red/yellow	4.2–6.3
Bromothymol blue	7.0	Yellow/blue	6.0–7.6
Phenolphthalein	9.3	Colourless/red	8.2–10.0

Phenol[A2]

Answer the questions and complete the grid to find a reagent that reacts readily with a solution of phenol at room temperature to form a white precipitate.

1   A hard, brittle phenol–methanal plastic discovered in 1905 and used for a long time for electrical insulation, saucepan handles and telephone casings.

2   A word to describe a plastic resin that sets hard on heating due to cross-linking.

3   Phenol dissolves in sodium hydroxide because the phenoxide ion is stabilised by bonding electrons of this kind.

4   A metal that reacts with molten phenol to form hydrogen and sodium phenoxide.

5   Phenol shows this property to a greater extent than C_2H_5OH, but to a lesser extent than CH_3CO_2H.

6   Chemicals, such as 2,4,6-trichlorophenol, that kill micro-organisms and can be used to disinfect wounds.

7   The type of substitution reaction that takes place more readily with phenol than with benzene.

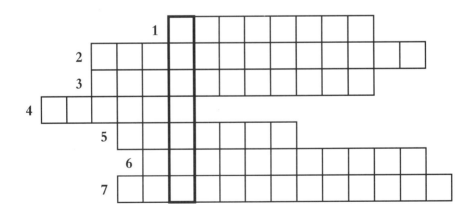

pK_a A2

Answer the questions with the help of this table of pK_a values.

Acid	pK_a value
sulfurous acid, H_2SO_3	1.8
hydrogensulfate ion, HSO_4^-	2.0
methanoic acid, CH_3CO_2H	3.8
ethanoic acid, $C_2H_5CO_2H$	4.8
chloric(I) acid, $HOCl$	6.4
carbonic acid, H_2CO_3	7.4
ammonium ion, NH_4^+	9.3
phenol, C_6H_5OH	9.9

1 What is the relationship between K_a and pK_a? ....

2 Which is the weakest acid in the table? ....

3 Which acid has the weakest conjugate base? ....

4 For which acid does $K_a = 0.01 \text{ mol dm}^{-3}$? ....

5 What is the pH of a solution containing equal concentrations of ethanoic acid and sodium ethanoate? ....

6 Name an acidic organic compound that produces carbon dioxide gas when added to sodium hydrogencarbonate solution. ....

7 Name an acidic organic compound that does not produce carbon dioxide gas when added to sodium hydrogencarbonate solution. ....

8 Suggest a suitable pair of compounds for making a buffer solution with pH = 4.

....

Polar covalent bonds[AS]

Indicate the polar bonds in these molecules with the help of the symbols δ+ and δ−.

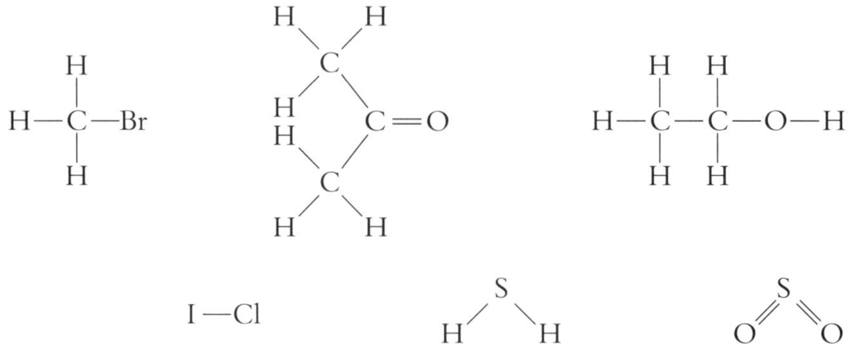

H—C—Br

(cyclopropane/carbonyl structure)

H—C—C—O—H

I—Cl

H—S—H

O=S=O

Polar molecules[AS]

Which of these molecules are overall polar and which are non-polar?

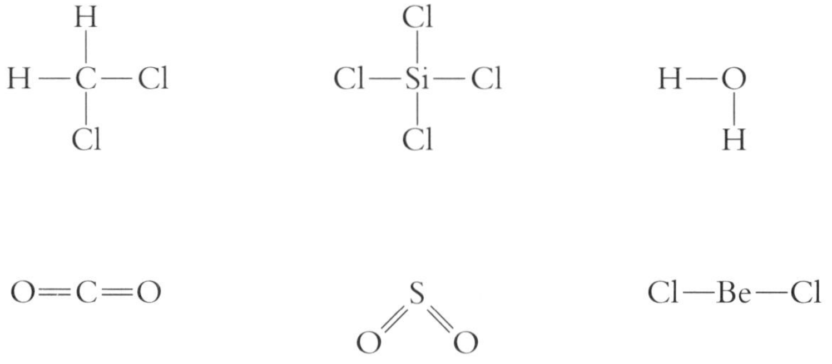

H—C—Cl

Cl—Si—Cl

H—O—H

O=C=O

O=S—O

Cl—Be—Cl

Proteins[A2]

Biochemists describe the structure of proteins at four levels: primary, secondary, tertiary or quaternary. Identify the level of structure for each of these descriptions

a	b ....
The sequence of amino acids in the polymer chains.	The three-dimensional folding of protein chains, which gives proteins, such as enzymes, a definite three-dimensional shape held in place by hydrogen bonding, disulfide bonds and interactions between amino acid side chains.
c	d ....
The ways in which the chains are arranged and held in place by hydrogen bonding within and between chains – this includes the coiling of chains in an α-helix in proteins such as keratin and the formation of layers of parallel chains as in the β-pleated sheets of silk.	The linking of two or more amino acid chains as in the hormone insulin, which consists of two chains linked by disulfide bonds.

Complete this diagram by drawing in the peptide group between the amino acids joining to form a dipeptide.

$$H_2N-\underset{\underset{H}{|}}{\overset{\overset{H_3C}{|}}{C}}- \qquad -\underset{\underset{H}{|}}{\overset{\overset{H}{|}}{C}}-CO_2H$$

Rate constant[A2]

Answer these questions.

1   The rate equation for the reaction of hydrogen with iodine forming hydrogen iodide is:

$$\text{rate} = k[H_2(g)][I_2(g)]$$

The rate constant is 8.6×10^{-5} dm^3 mol^{-1} s^{-1} at 375 K. Calculate the rate of reaction when the hydrogen concentration is 0.020 mol dm^{-3} and the concentration of iodine vapour is 0.040 mol dm^{-3}.

....

2   The hydrolysis of methyl ethanoate in alkali is first order with respect to both the ester and hydroxide ions. Write out the rate equation for this reaction. If the ester and hydroxide ion concentrations are both 0.020 mol dm^{-3}, calculate the rate of reaction at 298 K, given that the value of the rate constant is 0.14 dm^3 mol^{-1} s^{-1}.

....

Rate-determining step[A2]

Answer this question about rates and mechanisms.

The proposed mechanism for the reaction of aqueous solutions of ammonia and chlorate(I) ions has a sequence of three steps.

Fast step 1: $NH_3(aq) + OCl^-(aq) \rightarrow NH_2Cl(aq) + OH^-(aq)$

Slow step 2: $NH_2Cl(aq) + NH_3(aq) \rightarrow N_2H_5^+(aq) + Cl^-(aq)$

Fast step 3: $N_2H_5^+(aq) + OH^-(aq) \rightarrow N_2H_4(aq) + H_2O(l)$

a   What is the overall equation for the reaction? ....

b   Which is the rate-determining step? ....

c   Write a rate equation that is consistent with this proposed mechanism.

....

Rate equation[A2]

Write the balanced equation and the rate equation for the reactions listed below. In each case give the units of the rate constant, assuming that concentrations are measured in mol dm^{-3}.

1   The decomposition of gaseous ethanal to methane and carbon monoxide, which is second order with respect to ethanal.

    ....

    ....

2   The rearrangement of of cyclopropane gas to propene, which is first order with respect to cyclopropane.

    ....

    ....

3   The reaction of NO gas with bromine vapour to form NOBr gas which is first order with respect to bromine and second order with respect to NO.

    ....

    ....

4   The reaction of hydrogen with NO gas to give steam and nitrogen, given that, when the concentration of hydrogen doubles the rate doubles, but when the concentration of NO decreases by a factor of three, the rate falls by a factor of nine.

    ....

    ....

5   The decomposition of N_2O gas into its elements, given that the rate of reaction is proportional to the concentration of N_2O.

    ....

    ....

Rates of reaction[AS]

Connect each reaction in the left-hand column with the most suitable method for measuring its rate of reaction in the right-hand column by drawing a line. Assume that in each procedure measurements are taken at a series of time intervals.

Methods for studying rates

Reaction

Collecting and measuring the volume of a gas formed.

1

A $CH_3COCH_3(aq) + I_2(aq) \rightarrow$

$CH_3COCH_2I(aq) + H^+(aq) + I^-(aq)$

Removing measured samples of the mixture, stopping the reaction and then determining the concentration of one reactant or product by titration.

2

B $CaCO_3(s) + 2HCl(aq) \rightarrow$

$CaCl_2(aq) + CO_2(g) + H_2O(l)$

Using a colorimeter to follow the formation of a coloured product or the removal of a coloured reactant.

3

C $C_4H_9Br(l) + H_2O(l) \rightarrow$

$C_4H_9OH(aq) + H^+(aq) + Br^-(aq)$

Using a conductivity cell and meter to measure the changes in electrical conductivity of the reaction mixture as the number or nature of the ions changes.

4

D $CH_3CO_2CH_3(l) + H_2O(l) \rightarrow$

$CH_3CO_2H(l) + CH_3OH(l)$

Reaction mechanisms$^{AS/A2}$

Write equations for the following reactions, then give the name of the type of mechanism and the formula for the attacking species.

1   1-bromobutane with aqueous sodium hydroxide

....

Mechanism: ....

Attacking species: ....

2   Ethene with bromine

....

Mechanism: ....

Attacking species: ....

3   Propanone with potassium cyanide in the presence of acid

....

Mechanism: ....

Attacking species: ....

4   Ethane with chlorine

....

Mechanism: ....

Attacking species: ....

5   Benzene with a mixture of concentrated nitric and sulfuric acids

....

Mechanism: ....

Attacking species: ....

Recrystallisation[AS/A2]

These diagrams show stages in the purification of a solid organic compound by recrystallisation. Write down the letters for each stage in the correct order and state the purpose of each step.

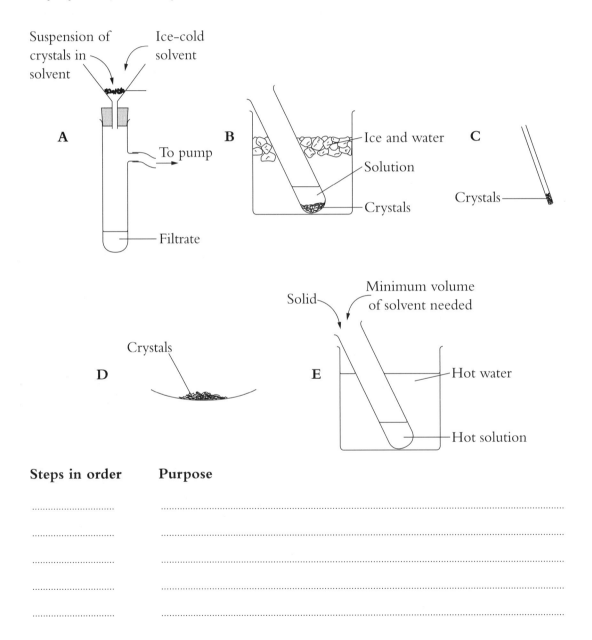

Steps in order	Purpose
....	....
....	....
....	....
....	....
....	....

Recycling[AS]

Pick from the grid statements relevant to the recycling of steel and then write the letters of the statements in a meaningful order. Now do the same for aluminium and then for plastics.

A Aluminium is not magnetic but can be separated from a waste stream by a rapidly varying magnetic field, which induces eddy currents in the metal of the can.	**B** Recycling steel can be done repeatedly because it is as good as new after reprocessing.	**C** Aluminium scrap from manufacturing processes is always recycled.	**D** Much of the recycled steel is waste from various stages of manufacturing steel objects, but some steel is recovered from the tin cans in household waste.	**E** The material used to make sparkling drink bottles, PET, is generally the most valuable. PET can be remelted and spun into fibres for carpets, bedding and clothing.
F Using recycled cans instead of the ore, bauxite, allows industry to make 20 times as many cans for the same amount of energy.	**G** An alternative approach to recycling plastics is to use cracking to produce a feedstock for oil refineries and chemical plants.	**H** The advantage of steel is that it is magnetic so that magnets can easily separate cans from other waste materials.	**I** Another plastic worth recycling is PVC, which can be recycled to make sewage pipes, flooring and even the soles of shoes.	**J** The interaction of the external field and the magnetic effect of the eddy currents leads to a force that can push cans out of the waste stream.
K Electric arc furnaces make steel plate, beams and bars by remelting nearly 100 per cent scrap steel.	**L** Less than 1 per cent of the mass of household waste is aluminium almost all of it in the form of drinks cans.	**M** Plastics are much more difficult to recycle than iron or steel.	**N** Worldwide, the steel industry recycles over 430 million tonnes of the metal each year, which is a recycling rate of over 50 per cent.	**O** There are many types of plastic that have to be sorted which is difficult, and plastics vary greatly in their value.

1   Recycling steel ....

2   Recycling aluminium ....

3   Recycling plastics ....

Redox reactions[AS]

Classify these substances as oxidising agents or as reducing agents based on their usual uses as reagents. Write the names of the elements or compounds into the appropriate column in the table: chlorine, bromine, hydrogen, hydrogen peroxide, iodine, nitric acid, oxygen, potassium dichromate(VI), potassium manganate(VII), sulfur dioxide, zinc with acid.

Oxidising agents	Reducing agents

Complete these pairs of half-equations by showing the numbers of electrons gained or lost. Then combine each pair of half equations to show the overall balanced equation.

$Fe^{3+}(aq) + \text{.............}e^- \rightarrow Fe^{2+}(aq)$

$2I^-(aq) \rightarrow I_2(aq) + \text{.............}e^-$

....

$I_2(aq) + \text{.............}e^- \rightarrow 2I^-(aq)$

$2S_2O_3^{2-}(aq) \rightarrow S_4O_6^{2-}(aq) + \text{.............}e^-$

....

$MnO_4^-(aq) + 8H^+(aq) + \text{.............}e^- \rightarrow Mn^{2+}(aq) + 4H_2O(l)$

$H_2O_2(aq) \rightarrow O_2(g) + 2H^+(aq) + \text{.............}e^-$

....

$Br_2(aq) + \text{.............}e^- \rightarrow 2Br^-(aq)$

$SO_2(aq) + 2H_2O(l) \rightarrow SO_4^{2-}(s) + 4H^+(aq) + \text{.............}e^-$

....

Redox titrations^A2

Complete this worked example.

> **Example:** A standard solution of potassium dichromate(VI) was prepared by dissolving 1.470 g in water and making the solution up to 250 cm³. Then 25.0 cm³ samples of the standard solution were added to excess potassium iodide and dilute sulfuric acid. In each case the iodine formed was titrated with the solution of sodium thiosulfate from a burette using starch as indicator. The average volume of sodium thiosulfate solution needed to decolourise the blue iodine–starch colour at the end-point was 30.00 cm³. Calculate the concentration of the solution of sodium thiosulfate standardised in this way.

ANSWER

Molar mass of potassium dichromate(VI), $K_2Cr_2O_7$ = ... g mol⁻¹

Amount of $K_2Cr_2O_7$ in the standard solution = 1.470 g ÷ .... g mol⁻¹

The volume of the standard solution = ... dm³

The concentration of the standard solution = (1.470 g ÷ .... g mol⁻¹) ÷ .... dm³

= .... mol dm⁻³

The equations for producing iodine:

$Cr_2O_7{}^{2-}$(aq) + ...I^-(aq) + ...H^+(aq) → $2Cr^{3+}$(aq) + ...I_2(aq) + $7H_2O$

The equation for the reaction during the titration:

I_2(aq) + ...$S_2O_3{}^{2-}$(aq) → $2I^-$(aq) + $S_4O_6{}^{2-}$(aq)

So 1 mol $Cr_2O_7{}^{2-}$ produces .... mol I_2 which reacts with .... mol $S_2O_3{}^{2-}$

Overall .... mol $S_2O_3{}^{2-}$ react with the iodine formed by 1 mol $Cr_2O_7{}^{2-}$

Amount of $Cr_2O_7{}^{2-}$(aq) in the 25 cm³ sample in the flask at the start

= .... dm³ × .... mol dm⁻³

So the amount of thiosulfate in 30.00 cm³ = ... dm³ solution

= .... × (............... dm³ × ....mol dm⁻³)

So the concentration of the sodium thiosulfate solution

= [........... × (........... dm³ × .... mol dm⁻³)] ÷ .... dm³ = ... mol dm⁻³

Reversible reactions[AS]

Write into the arrows above and below these equations a change in conditions which can make these reversible reactions go in one direction or the other.

a

c

b

d

$N_2(g) + 3H_2(g) \rightleftharpoons 2NH_3(g)$ $\Delta H^{\ominus} = -92$ kJ mol^{-1} $Br_2(aq) + H_2O(l) \rightleftharpoons HOBr(aq) + Br^-(aq) + H^+(aq)$

Shapes of molecules[AS]

Underneath each of these dot-and-cross diagrams sketch a diagram to show the shape of the molecule and estimate the size of the bond angles in each molecule.

Skeletal formulae[AS]

Give the molecular formula, structural formula and name for each of the compounds with the skeletal formulae shown.

A

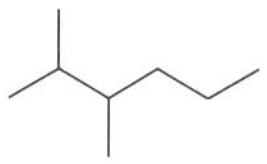

B

C

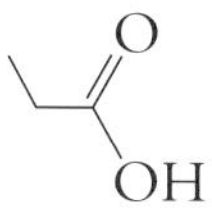

D

E

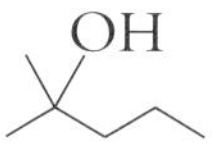

F

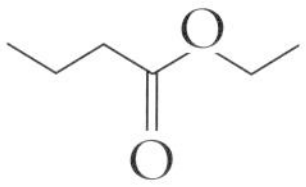

Stability[A2]

Complete the right-hand column of this table by stating in each situation whether the reactants are stable (energetically or kinetically) or unstable relative to the products.

$\Delta G \approx \Delta H$	Activation energy	Change observed	Stability
Positive	High	No reaction	
Negative	High	No reaction	
Positive	Low	No reaction	
Negative	Low	Fast reaction	

Structural isomerism[AS]

CHAIN ISOMERISM

Draw and name the structures of the chain isomers that are alkanes with four carbon atoms.

POSITION ISOMERISM

Draw and name the structures of two position isomers of alcohols with three carbon atoms.

FUNCTIONAL GROUP ISOMERISM

Draw and name two functional group isomers with the molecular formula C_3H_6O.

Sulfuric acid manufacture^{AS}

Decide on the correct sequence for the separate parts of a flow diagram to describe the manufacture of sulfuric acid. Enter the letters in the sequence of boxes.

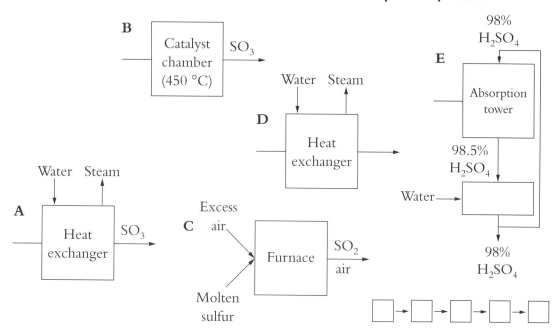

Complete the chemical equations for the reactions in the main parts of the process.

In the furnace: ....( ) + O_2( ) → ....( )

In the catalyst chamber: ....(g) + O_2(g) ....(g) $\Delta H = -197$ kJ mol^{-1}

In the absorption tower: ....( ) + ... (l) → H_2SO_4(l)

The catalyst is: ....

Features of the process which speed up the reaction:

....

....

Features of the process which favour the conversion of reactants to products as the mixture of gases pass through the four layers of catalyst:

....

....

Tests for organic functional groups[A2]

Match the organic compounds in the left-hand column with the results of chemical tests in the right-hand column. Draw a line from each number to the appropriate letter.

Compound		*Test*	
Propene	1	A	A liquid that gives a silver mirror with Tollen's reagent and an orange precipitate with and acidified solution of 2,4-dinitrophenylhydrazine (Brady's reagent).
1-Bromopropane	2	B	A liquid that gives an acidic solution in water that reacts with sodium carbonate to produce carbon dioxide.
Propan-1-ol	3	C	Refluxing with excess potassium dichromate(VI) produces a mixture of products from which it is possible to distil a colourless, acidic liquid.
Propan-2-ol	4	D	A neutral liquid that gives off fumes of an acid gas when mixed with PCl_5, but does not react on heating with an acidic solution of potassium dichromate(VI).
2-Methylpropan-2-ol	5	E	A cream-coloured precipitate forms after warming a few drops of this liquid with aqueous sodium hydroxide, acidifying with dilute nitric acid and then adding silver nitrate solution.
Propanal	6	F	A gas that decolourises an aqueous solution of bromine.
Propanone	7	G	A neutral liquid that gives an orange precipitate with an acidified of 2,4-dinitrophenylhydrazine, but does not reduce Fehling's solution.
Propanoic acid	8	H	Potassium dichromate(VI) turns from orange to green on heating with this liquid and a neutral product distils from the reaction mixture. The product does not react with Tollen's reagent.

Transition metals[A2]

Identify the transition metal that has the properties described. You can name the same element more than once.

1   The element with the electron configuration: $1s^2 2s^2 2p^6 3s^2 3p^6 3d^{10} 4s^1$. ....

2   A grey metal used to make spatulas and crucibles as well as being one of the components of the magnetic alloy, Alnico. ....

3   A metal that forms ions with these oxidation states and ions in aqueous solution: +2 (violet), +3 (green), +4 (blue) and +5 (yellow). ....

4   A metal that forms a brick-red oxide and a white chloride in the +1 state. ....

5   A metal that, in the +3 state, form a deep red complex with CNS^- ions in aqueous solution. ....

6   A metal that forms a pale blue aquo complex, which undergoes ligand exchange with ammonia to form a deep blue complex. ....

7   An element that forms a pale green aquo complex in the +2 state, which is oxidised by oxygen or chlorine to a yellow aquo complex in the +3 state. ....

8   An element that forms oxo- ions in the +7 state, which act as a powerful oxidising agent in acid solution. ....

9   Adding sodium hydroxide solution to a solution of the ions of this element in the +3 state produces a green precipitate that dissolves in excess alkali. ....

10   This metal forms an oxide in the +5 state, used as a catalyst in the manufacture of SO_3 from SO_2. ....

11   This metal is the catalyst for the manufacture of ammonia from nitrogen and hydrogen. ....

12   This metal is the catalyst for the hydrogenation of vegetable oils. ....

Ultraviolet and visible spectroscopy[A2]

For each of these analyses, state whether you would use ultraviolet (UV) or visible spectroscopy.

1   To determine the concentration of a solution of paracetamol (N-ethanoyl-4-aminophenol) ....

2   To find the ratio of copper(II) ions to EDTA in a complex ion ....

3   To investigate the energy levels for electrons in benzene ....

4   To measure the concentration of ozone in the air ....

5   To measure the concentration of iron(III) ions in the presence of CNS⁻ ions
    ....

6   To estimate the equilibrium constant for the ionisation of an acid–base indicator
    ....

The visible region of the spectrum runs from 400 nm (violet) to 700 nm (red). Match these absorption spectra with these aqueous ions: Cu^{2+}, Co^{2+}, $Cr_2O_7^{2-}$ and Ni^{2+}.

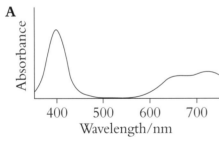

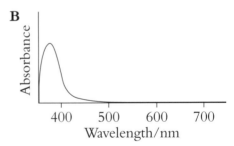

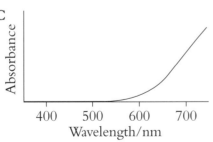

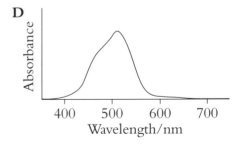

Yield calculations^{AS/A2}

Suggest three reasons why the yield from a chemical synthesis may be less than the theoretical yield predicted by the chemical equation.

1 ....

2 ....

3 ....

Calculate the theoretical yield and percentage yield for these examples.

4   A synthesis of aluminium chloride from 5.4 g aluminium and excess chlorine gas produced 23.4 g product.

Theoretical yield = ...

Percentage yield = ...

5   A synthesis of ethanamide from 52 g ethanoic acid by converting the acid to its ammonium salt and then heating the salt gave 15 g of product.

Theoretical yield = ...

Percentage yield = ...

PHYSICAL CHEMISTRY MULTIPLE CHOICE TEST^{A2}

MULTIPLE CHOICE QUESTIONS

In questions 1–17 choose the ONE BEST answer.

1   The first five ionisation energies of an element in kJ mol^{-1} are:

419, 3051, 4412, 5877, 7975. The element is in:

A   group 1

B   group 2

C   group 3

D   group 4

2   Which of these sets of properties is that of an ionic compound?

	Electrical conductivity when solid	Electrical conductivity when liquid	Melting point
A	good	good	63 °C
B	good	good	650 °C
C	poor	poor	8.4 °C
D	poor	good	712 °C

3   In which of these molecules do the intermolecular forces arise largely from attractions between temporary dipoles?

A NH_3

B   HBr

C CH_2Br_2

D N_2

4   Which of these reactions is an acid–base reaction?

A $H_2(g) + Cl_2(g) \rightarrow 2HCl(g)$

B $N_2(g) + 3H_2(g) \rightarrow 2NH_3(g)$

C $NH_3(g) + HCl(g) \rightarrow NH_4Cl(aq)$

D $HCl(aq) + AgNO_3(aq) \rightarrow AgCl(s) + HNO_3(aq)$

5 The results in the table refer to the decomposition of ethanal to methane and carbon monoxide.

Initial concentration of ethanal/ mol dm^{-3}	Initial rate of reaction/ mol dm^{-3} s^{-1}
0.10	0.02
0.20	0.08
0.30	0.18

What is the order of reaction with respect to ethanal?

A 0

B 1

C 2

D 3

6 Nitrogen monoxide reacts with oxygen:

$$2NO(g) + O_2(g) \rightarrow 2NO_2(g)$$

The reaction is second order with respect to NO and first order with respect to oxygen. The rate of change of the NO concentration is 7×10^{-6} mol dm^{-3} s^{-1} when the initial concentrations of both NO and O_2 are 0.001 mol dm^{-3}. What is the rate of reaction when [NO] = 0.002 mol dm^{-3} and [O_2] = 0.003 mol dm^{-3}.

A 21×10^{-6} mol dm^{-3} s^{-1}

B 42×10^{-6} mol dm^{-3} s^{-1}

C 84×10^{-6} mol dm^{-3} s^{-1}

D 126×10^{-6} mol dm^{-3} s^{-1}

7 If pressure is measured in pascals (Pa), what are the units of K_p for this equilibrium?

$$2SO_2(g) + O_2(g) \rightleftharpoons 2SO_3(g)$$

A Pa^2

B Pa^{-1}

C Pa

D no units

8 Which of these changes alters the value of the equilibrium constant for a reaction between gases?

A changing the pressure

B changing the concentration of one reactant

C changing the temperature

D adding a catalyst

Answer questions 9–13 with the help of this information.

Half cell	$E^{\ominus}_{cell}/V$	Half cell	$E^{\ominus}_{cell}/V$
$Pt(H_2)\|2H^+(aq)\vdots Ag^+(aq)\|Ag(s)$	+0.80	$Pt(H_2)\|2H^+(aq)\vdots Fe^{2+}(aq)\|Fe(s)$	−0.44
$Pt(H_2)\|2H^+(aq)\vdots Br_2(aq), 2Br^-(aq)\|Pt$	+1.09	$Pt(H_2)\|2H^+(aq)\vdots Fe^{3+}(aq), Fe^{2+}(aq)\|Pt$	+0.77
$Pt(H_2)\|2H^+(aq)\vdots Cu^+(aq)\|Cu(s)$	+0.52	$Pt(H_2)\|2H^+(aq)\vdots I_2(aq),2I^-(aq)\|Pt$	+0.54
$Pt(H_2)\|2H^+(aq)\vdots Cu^{2+}(aq)\|Cu^+(aq)$	+0.15	$Pt(H_2)\|2H^+(aq)\vdots Sn^{2+}(aq)\|Sn(s)$	−0.14
$Pt(H_2)\|2H^+(aq)\vdots Cu^{2+}(aq)\|Cu(s)$	+0.34	$Pt(H_2)\|2H^+(aq)\vdots Zn^{2+}(aq)\|Zn(s)$	−0.76

9   What is the standard electrode potential of an electrode made by dipping copper metal into a $1.0 \ mol \ dm^{-3}$ solution of copper(II) sulfate under standard conditions?

    A $-0.34 \ V$

    B $+0.34 \ V$

    C $-0.15 \ V$

    D $+0.15 \ V$

10   What is the emf of this cell: $Zn(s)\|Zn^{2+}(aq) \ \vdots \ Fe^{2+}(aq)\|Fe(s)$?

    A $+0.32 \ V$

    B $-0.32 \ V$

    C $+1.2 \ V$

    D $-1.2 \ V$

11   Which is the strongest reducing agent of all the species shown in the table of data?

    A bromine molecules

    B bromide ions

    C zinc metal

    D zinc ions

12   Which of these reactions tends to go from left to right?

    A $2Fe^{3+}(aq) + 2I^-(aq) \rightarrow 2Fe^{2+}(aq) + I_2(aq)$

    B $2Ag(s) + Sn^{2+}(aq) \rightarrow 2Ag^+(aq) + Sn(s)$

    C $Cu^{2+}(aq) + 2Fe^{2+}(aq) \rightarrow Cu(s) + 2Fe^{3+}(aq)$

    D $Sn(s) + Zn^{2+}(aq) \rightarrow Sn^{2+}(aq) + Zn(s)$

13 Which of these ions tends to disproportionate?

A Cu^+

B Fe^{2+}

C Cu^{2+}

D Fe^{3+}

14 K_a for methanoic acid $= 1.6 \times 10^{-4}$ mol dm^{-3} (p$K_a = 3.8$). During a titration of 20.0 cm^3 0.1 mol dm^{-3} methanoic acid with 0.1 mol dm^{-3} sodium hydroxide, the hydrogen ion concentration $= 1.6 \times 10^{-4}$ mol dm^{-3} (pH $= 3.8$) when the volume of alkali added from the burette is:

A 0.0 cm^3

B 10.0 cm^3

C 20.0 cm^3

D 30.0 cm^3

15 Which indicator is suitable for detecting the end-point of a titration of 0.1 mol dm^{-3} ethanoic acid with 0.1 mol dm^{-3} sodium hydroxide?

A Thymolphthalein (p$K_a = 9.7$)

B Bromophenol blue (p$K_a = 4.0$)

C Thymol blue (p$K_a = 1.7$)

D Methyl violet (p$K_a = 0.8$)

16 The energy needed to atomise 1 mol of gaseous ethene, C_2H_4, is $+2087$ kJ mol^{-1}. The bond enthalpy for the C=C bond is $+347$ kJ mol^{-1}. So the average bond enthalpy for a C—H bond is:

A $+348$ kJ mol^{-1}

B $+435$ kJ mol^{-1}

C $+696$ kJ mol^{-1}

D $+870$ kJ mol^{-1}

17 For which of these changes is the enthalpy change the lattice enthalpy of potassium chloride?

A $K^+(g) + Cl^-(g) \rightarrow KCl(s)$

B $K(s) + \frac{1}{2}Cl_2(g) \rightarrow KCl(s)$

C $KOH(aq) + HCl(aq) \rightarrow KCl(aq) + H_2O(l)$

D $K^+(g) + Cl^-(g) + aq \rightarrow K^+(aq) + Cl^-(aq)$

MULTIPLE COMPLETION QUESTIONS

Questions 18–30 are multiple completion items. For each multiple completion question ONE or MORE of the responses given is/are correct. Decide which of the responses is/are correct. Then refer to the table to select your answer A, B, C or D.

Summarised directions for multiple completion questions			
A (i), (ii) and (iii) only	**B** (i) and (iii) only	**C** (ii) and (iv) only	**D** (iv) only

18 Which of these consist of polar molecules?

(i)   carbon dioxide

(ii)   steam

(iii)   beryllium chloride vapour

(iv)   sulfur dioxide

19 Which of these elements consist of a giant structure of atoms joined by covalent bonding?

(i)   silicon

(ii)   sulfur

(iii)   carbon (diamond)

(iv)   iodine

20 Which of these changes are redox reactions?

(i) $KCl(s) + H_2SO_4(l) \rightarrow HCl(g) + KHSO_4(s)$

(ii) $CH_3NH_2(g) + HCl(g) \rightarrow CH_3NH_3Cl(s)$

(iii) $ZnCO_3(s) \rightarrow ZnO(s) + CO_2(g)$

(iv) $2HBr(g) + H_2SO_4(l) \rightarrow Br_2(l) + SO_2(g) + 2H_2O(l)$

21 The rate at which a mixture of ethanol and ethanoic acid reaches equilibrium is affected by:

(i)   the presence of an acid catalyst

(ii)   the concentration of the reactants

(iii)   the temperature

(iv)   the value of K_c

Summarised directions for multiple completion questions			
A	**B**	**C**	**D**
(i), (ii) and (iii) only	(i) and (iii) only	(ii) and (iv) only	(iv) only

22 Mixing iron(II) chloride solution with silver nitrate solution produces a precipitate of silver and forms this equilibrium mixture:

$$Fe^{2+}(aq) + Ag^+(aq) \rightleftharpoons Fe^{3+}(aq) + Ag(s)$$

After decanting the aqueous layer, the silver can be redissolved by adding an aqueous solution of:
(i)   sodium chloride
(ii)   iron(II) chloride
(iii) silver nitrate
(iv)   iron(III) chloride

23 The reaction of iron with steam is exothermic. In a closed container at 700 °C this equation describes the equilibrium:

$$3Fe(s) + 4H_2O(g) \rightleftharpoons Fe_3O_4(s) + 4H_2(g)$$

The proportion of hydrogen in the equilibrium mixture is increased by:
(i)   increasing the mass of iron
(ii)   increasing the pressure
(iii) decreasing the mass of Fe_3O_4
(iv)   decreasing the temperature

24 Which of these species can act as both acids and as bases in aqueous solution?
(i) H_2O
(ii) OH^-
(iii) HCO_3^-
(iv) $CH_3CO_2^-$

25 The pH = 3.4 for a 0.01 mol dm^{-3} solution of an acid. The acid could be:
(i)   HCl
(ii) H_2SO_4
(iii) HNO_3
(iv) $CH_3CH_2CO_2H$

Summarised directions for multiple completion questions			
A (i), (ii) and (iii) only	**B** (i) and (iii) only	**C** (ii) and (iv) only	**D** (iv) only

26 Which of these mixtures in aqueous solution can be used as a buffer solution?
   (i)   Sodium hydroxide and ammonia
   (ii) Sodium carbonate and sodium hydrogencarbonate
   (iii) Ammonium chloride and hydrochloric acid
   (iv) Sodium ethanoate and ethanoic acid

27 Which of these enthalpy changes features in the Born–Haber cycle to calculate the lattice enthalpy of magnesium oxide?
   (i)   first and second ionisation enthalpies of magnesium
   (ii) standard enthalpy change of formation of magnesium oxide
   (iii) enthalpies of atomisation of magnesium and oxygen
   (iv) first and second ionisation enthalpies of oxygen

28 Which of these quantities increase from left to right along the series:

   $MgSO_4$, $CaSO_4$, $SrSO_4$, $BaSO_4$?
   (i)   Lattice enthalpy of the compounds
   (ii) Hydration enthalpy of the metal ions
   (iii) Solubility of the salts
   (iv) Size of the metal ion

29 Which of these quantities do chemists use to predict the direction and extent of chemical change?
   (i)   Equilibrium constant, K_c
   (ii) Activation energy, E_a
   (iii) Standard emf of a cell, $E^{\ominus}_{cell}$
   (iv) Rate constant, k

30 There is no reaction in these mixtures at room temperature and pressure. For which of the mixtures is the lack of reaction due to kinetic stability?
   (i)   nitrogen and oxygen
   (ii) methane and oxygen
   (iii) aluminium oxide and carbon dioxide
   (iv) aluminium metal and air

INORGANIC CHEMISTRY MULTIPLE CHOICE TEST^{A2}

MULTIPLE CHOICE QUESTIONS

In questions 1–13 choose the ONE BEST answer.

1 Which is the electron configuration of a transition element with the highest oxidation state +7?
  A $1s^22s^22p^63s^23p^5$
  B $1s^22s^22p^63s^23p^63d^14s^2$
  C $1s^22s^22p^63s^23p^63d^54s^2$
  D $1s^22s^22p^63s^23p^63d^74s^2$

2 In which of these molecules do the intermolecular forces arise largely from attractions between permanent dipoles?
  A I_2
  B CCl_4
  C CH_3Br
  D SiH_4

3 Iodine oxidises thiosulfate ions, $S_2O_3^{2-}$, to:
  A SO_2
  B SO_3^{2-}
  C SO_4^{2-}
  D $S_4O_6^{2-}$

4 Adding aqueous sodium hydroxide to one sample of a solution of a salt produces a rusty-brown precipitate. Adding dilute nitric acid followed by silver nitrate to another sample of the solution produces a white precipitate. The salt in the solution is:
  A   iron(II) sulfate
  B   iron(II) chloride
  C   iron(III) sulfate
  D   iron(III) chloride

5   Chlorine disproportionates when it reacts with:

   A   water

   B   aluminium

   C   silicon

   D   magnesium

6   Which of these chlorides dissolves in water to give a neutral solution?

   A $MgCl_2$

   B $AlCl_3$

   C $SiCl_4$

   D PCl_3

7   Which of these oxides is amphoteric?

   A MgO

   B Al_2O_3

   C SiO_2

   D SO_2

8   Which of these complex ions has an octahedral shape?

   A $[Ag(NH_3)_2]^+$

   B $[CuCl_4]^{2-}$

   C $[Pt(NH_3)_4]^{2+}$

   D $[Mn(H_2O)_6]^{2+}$

9   What volume of $0.010 \ mol \ dm^{-3} \ MnO_4^-(aq)$ is required to oxidise $20.0 \ cm^3$ of $0.04 \ mol \ dm^{-3} \ Fe^{2+}(aq)$?

   A $80.0 \ cm^3$

   B $25.0 \ cm^3$

   C $16.0 \ cm^3$

   D $4.0 \ cm^3$

10 What is the pattern of melting points of the elements across period 3?

   A   Melting points rise from left to right across the period.

   B   Melting points fall from left to right across the period.

   C   Melting points fall from sodium to silicon, then they rise sharply to phosphorus and remain high for the other non-metals in the period.

   D   Melting points rise from sodium to silicon, then they fall sharply to phosphorus and remain low for the other non-metals in the period.

11 Under what conditions can hydrogen peroxide oxidise cobalt(II) to cobalt(III) according to these standard electrode potentials?

$$[Co(H_2O)_6]^{3+}(aq) + e^- \rightleftharpoons [Co(H_2O)_6]^{2+}(aq) \qquad E^{\ominus} = +1.82\,V$$

$$[Co(NH_3)_6]^{3+}(aq) + e^- \rightleftharpoons [Co(NH_3)_6]^{2+}(aq) \qquad E^{\ominus} = +0.10\,V$$

$$H_2O_2(aq) + 2H^+(aq) + 2e^- \rightleftharpoons 2H_2O(l) \qquad E^{\ominus} = +1.77\,V$$

A In dilute aqueous solution

B In the presence of excess ammonia

C In the presence of excess hydrochloric acid

D In the presence of excess sodium hydroxide

12 In which of these molecules do all of the atoms lie in the same plane?

A NH_3

B PCl_3

C BCl_3

D SO_3

13 Which chemical species is quickly oxidised by a warm, acidic solution of potassium dichromate(VI)?

A $(CH_3)_3COH$

B CH_3CO_2H

C Fe^{2+}

D Zn^{2+}

MULTIPLE COMPLETION QUESTIONS

Questions 14–30 are multiple completion items. For each multiple completion question, ONE or MORE of the responses given is/are correct. Decide which of the responses is/are correct. Then refer to the table to select your answer A, B, C or D.

Summarised directions for multiple completion questions			
A (i), (ii) and (iii) only	**B** (i) and (iii) only	**C** (ii) and (iv) only	**D** (iv) only

14 Which of these compounds in the solid state contain ions?

  (i) K_2O

  (ii) NH_4Br

  (iii) HCO_2Na

  (iv) SiO_2

15 Dative covalent (coordinate) bonding is involved in the formation of:

  (i) NH_4^+

  (ii) $[Cu(H_2O)_6]^{2+}$

  (iii) H_3O^+

  (iv) CH_3CO_2H

16 Which of the statements about these ions are true?

$N^{3-}, O^{2-}, F^-, Na^+, Mg^{2+}$

  (i)   They all have the same electron configuration

  (ii) The ionic radii increase from left to right along the series

  (iii) They are isoelectronic with a neon atom

  (iv) The ions are larger than the atoms from which they formed

17 Tetrachloromethane and silicon tetrachloride both:

  (i)   consist of non-polar molecules

  (ii) form when chlorine reacts with the non-metal on heating

  (iii) are colourless liquids at room temperature and pressure

  (iv) are rapidly hydrolysed by water

Summarised directions for multiple completion questions			
A (i), (ii) and (iii) only	**B** (i) and (iii) only	**C** (ii) and (iv) only	**D** (iv) only

18 Which of the following increase down group 2 from magnesium to barium?
   (i)   thermal stability of the carbonates
   (ii)   thermal stability of the nitrates
   (iii) solubility of the hydroxides in water
   (iv)   solubility of the sulfates in water

19 Which of the following increase down group 7 from chlorine to iodine?
   (i)   electronegativity
   (ii)   boiling point
   (iii) strength as an oxidising agent
   (iv)   covalent radius of the atoms

20 Which of the following increase from left to right along the series:

$$AgCl - AgBr - AgI?$$

   (i)   intensity of colour
   (ii)   solubility in water
   (iii) ease of oxidation to the halogen
   (iv)   solubility in aqueous ammonia.

21 Hydrogen is reduced when it reacts with:
   (i)   oxygen to form water
   (ii)   nitrogen to form ammonia
   (iii) chlorine to form hydrogen chloride
   (iv)   sodium to form sodium hydride

22 Which of these changes are disproportionation reactions?
   (i) $2Cu^+(aq) \rightarrow Cu^{2+}(aq) + Cu(s)$
   (ii) $2H_2O_2(aq) \rightarrow H_2O(l) + \frac{1}{2}O_2(g)$
   (iii) $Cl_2(aq) + NaOH(aq) \rightarrow NaOCl(aq) + NaCl(aq)$
   (iv) $Fe^{3+}(aq) + Fe(s) \rightarrow 2Fe^{2+}(aq)$

Summarised directions for multiple completion questions			
A (i), (ii) and (iii) only	**B** (i) and (iii) only	**C** (ii) and (iv) only	**D** (iv) only

23 In which of these complex ions is the oxidation state of the metal $+2$?

(i) $[Fe(CN)_6]^{4-}$

(ii) $[Cu(NH_3)_4(H_2O)_2]^{2+}$

(iii) $[CoCl_4]^{2-}$

(iv) $[Fe(H_2O)_5(SCN)]^{2+}$

24 Which of these is an example of homogeneous catalysis?

(i)   hydrogenation of a vegetable oil in the presence of nickel

(ii) oxidation of ammonia to oxides of nitrogen in the presence of platinum

(iii) oxidation of sulfur dioxide to sulfur trioxide in the presence of vanadium(v) oxide

(iv) oxidation of aqueous iodide ions by aqueous peroxodisulfate(vi) ions in the presence of iron(ii) ions

25 In which of these complex ions is there a bidentate ligand?

(i) $[PtCl_2(NH_3)_2]$

(ii) $[Ag(NH_3)_2]^+$

(iii) $[Cu(NH_3)_4(H_2O)_2]^{2+}$

(iv) $[Fe(C_2O_4)_3]^{3-}$

26 Which of these changes leading to a change of colour involve both a change of oxidation state and a change of ligand?

(i)   blue to green: $[Cr(H_2O)_6]^{2+} \rightarrow [Cr(H_2O)_6]^{3+}$

(ii) pale blue to deep blue: $[Cu(H_2O)_6]^{2+} \rightarrow [Cu(NH_3)_4(H_2O)_2]^{2+}$

(iii) pink to blue: $[Co(H_2O)_6]^{2+} \rightarrow [CoCl_4]^{2-}$

(iv) pale green to yellow: $[Fe(H_2O)_6]^{2+} \rightarrow [Fe(H_2O)_5OH]^{2+}$

27 Ammonia acts as:

(i)   a base when it dissolves in water

(ii) a ligand when added to copper(ii) sulfate solution

(iii) a nucleophile when it reacts with 1-bromobutane

(iv) an oxidising agent when it reacts with chlorine

Summarised directions for multiple completion questions			
A	**B**	**C**	**D**
(i), (ii) and (iii) only	(i) and (iii) only	(ii) and (iv) only	(iv) only

28 Which of these species can be oxidised?

(i) Fe^{2+}

(ii) Zn^{2+}

(iii) VO^{2+}

(iv) MnO_4^-

29 A precipitate of a metal carbonate forms on adding sodium carbonate solution to an aqueous solution containing:

(i) Fe^{3+}

(ii) Cu^{2+}

(iii) Al^{3+}

(iv) Zn^{2+}

30 The polarising power of the simple metal ions increases:

(i) across period 3 from Na^+ to Al^{3+}

(ii) down group 2 from Mg^{2+} to Ba^{2+}

(iii) as the oxidation state of Fe increases from $+2$ to $+3$

(iv) down group 1 from Li^+ to Cs^+

ORGANIC CHEMISTRY MULTIPLE CHOICE TEST[A2]

MULTIPLE CHOICE QUESTIONS

In questions 1–16 choose the ONE BEST answer.

1   One of the temperatures A to D is the true boiling point of 2-methylpentane. Select the temperature that is most likely to be correct.

Alkane	Boiling point/°C
Pentane	36
Hexane	69
2,2-dimethylpropane	10
2,2-dimethylbutane	50

   A   22 °C
   B   44 °C
   C   60 °C
   D   75 °C

2   One mole of a hydrocarbon $C_{10}H_{14}$ absorbs two moles of hydrogen in the presence of a platinum catalyst to give a product that does not react with a dilute solution of bromine. How many rings are there in the structure of the hydrocarbon?
   A   1
   B   2
   C   3
   D   4

3   A sample of hexane contaminated by hex-3-ene can be purified by shaking with concentrated sulfuric acid. The sulfuric acid:
   A   absorbs the hexane but not the hex-3-ene
   B   absorbs the hex-3-ene but not the hexane
   C   converts hex-3-ene to hexane
   D   dehydrates hexane to hex-3-ene

4   Choose the alkene which polymerises to give this structure:

$$---\!\!-\overset{\displaystyle CH_3}{\underset{\displaystyle H}{\overset{|}{\underset{|}{C}}}}\!\!-\!\!\overset{\displaystyle H}{\underset{\displaystyle H}{\overset{|}{\underset{|}{C}}}}\!\!-\!\!\overset{\displaystyle CH_3}{\underset{\displaystyle H}{\overset{|}{\underset{|}{C}}}}\!\!-\!\!\overset{\displaystyle H}{\underset{\displaystyle H}{\overset{|}{\underset{|}{C}}}}\!\!-\!\!\overset{\displaystyle CH_3}{\underset{\displaystyle H}{\overset{|}{\underset{|}{C}}}}\!\!-\!\!\overset{\displaystyle H}{\underset{\displaystyle H}{\overset{|}{\underset{|}{C}}}}\!\!-\!\!\overset{\displaystyle CH_3}{\underset{\displaystyle H}{\overset{|}{\underset{|}{C}}}}\!\!-\!\!\overset{\displaystyle H}{\underset{\displaystyle H}{\overset{|}{\underset{|}{C}}}}\!\!-\!\!---$$

   A   methylpropene

   B   but-2-ene

   C   but-1-ene

   D   propene

5   A mixture of potassium bromide and sulfuric acid converts ethanol to bromoethane. What is the theoretical yield from 8.0 g ethanol, 18.0 g sulfuric acid and 12.0 g potassium bromide?

   A   11.0 g

   B   13.1 g

   C   19.0 g

   D   20.0 g

6   Which of these pairs of substances react to give bromoethane as the only product?

   A   ethane and bromine

   B   ethene and bromine

   C   ethene and hydrogen bromide

   D   ethanol and hydrogen bromide

7   When preparing propanal by oxidising of propan-1-ol with acidified potassium dichromate(VI), it is necessary to ensure that the oxidising agent is never in excess and to distil off the aldehyde as it forms. If these precautions are not taken, the reaction produces:

   A   propanoic acid

   B   propanone

   C   propene

   D   carbon dioxide and water

8   If ethyl ethanoate is heated under reflux with an excess of aqueous sodium hydroxide and the resulting solution is then distilled, the distillate contains:

   A   ethanol only

   B   ethanoic acid and water only

   C   ethanol and water only

   D   ethanol, ethanoic acid and water

9 What is the sequence of types of change in this synthesis?

$$CH_3-CH=CH_2 \xrightarrow{Br_2} CH_3-CHBr-CH_2Br \xrightarrow[H^+]{KCN} CH_3-\underset{\underset{CN}{|}}{CH}-CH_2CN \xrightarrow{H_2O/H^+} CH_3-\underset{\underset{\underset{O}{\|}{C}}{|}}{CH}-CH_2-C\overset{O}{\underset{OH}{\diagdown}}$$

A addition – substitution – hydrolysis – esterification

B addition – hydrolysis – substitution – esterification

C substitution – addition – esterification – hydrolysis

D substitution – esterification – addition – hydrolysis

$$\downarrow C_2H_5OH/H^+$$

$$CH_3-\underset{\underset{\underset{O}{\|}{C}}{|}}{CH}-CH_2-C\overset{O}{\underset{OC_2H_5}{\diagdown}}$$

10 Identify the reagents P and Q in this two-step synthesis

	P	Q
A	$NO_2(g)$	$LiAlH_4(s)$
B	$HNO_2(aq)$	$H_2(g)/Pt(s)$
C	$HNO_3(aq)$	$H_2(g)/Ni(s)$
D	$HNO_3(l)/H_2SO_4(l)$	$Sn/HCl(aq)$

11 Which of these amino acids occurs in naturally occurring proteins?

A $H_2N-CH_2-CH_2-CH_2-CH_2-CH_2-CH_2-CO_2H$

B $CH_3-\underset{\underset{NH_2}{|}}{\overset{\overset{CH_3}{|}}{C}}-CH_2-CO_2H$

C $H_2N-CH_2-CH_2-CO_2H$

D $CH_3-\underset{\underset{NH_2}{|}}{CH}-CO_2H$

12 Which of these reactions is an example of a nucleophilic addition reaction?

A $CH_3CH_2CH_2Br + CN^- \rightarrow CH_3CH_2CH_2CN + Br^-$

B $CH_3COCH_3 + HCN \rightarrow CH_3COH(CN)CH_3$

C $CH_3CHCH_2 + HBr \rightarrow CH_3CHBrCH_3$

D $C_6H_6 + Br_2 \rightarrow C_6H_5Br + HBr$

13 Which of these reactions produces a mixture of the optical isomers of a compound?

    A $CH_3CH_2CH_2Br + CN^- \rightarrow CH_3CH_2CH_2CN + Br^-$

    B $CH_3COCH_3 + HCN \rightarrow CH_3COH(CN)CH_3$

    C $CH_3CH{=}CH_2 + HBr \rightarrow CH_3CHBrCH_3$

    D $C_6H_6 + Br_2 \rightarrow C_6H_5Br + HBr$

14 A reagent which can be used to distinguish butanal from butanone is:

    A   a solution of bromine in hexane

    B   Fehling's solution

    C PCl_5

    D   sodium metal

15 Identify a compound for which this could be the mass spectrum.

    A CH_3Br

    B CH_2Cl_2

    C $C_6H_5CH_3$

    D C_6H_5OH

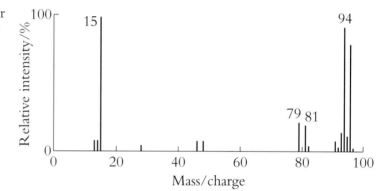

16 With the help of the table of chemical shifts, identify the structure of the compound C_4H_8O for which this could be the low resolution nmr spectrum.

    A $CH_2{=}CHCH_2CH_2OH$

    B $CH_3CH_2CH_2CHO$

    C $(CH_3)_2CHCHO$

    D $CH_3CH_2COCH_3$

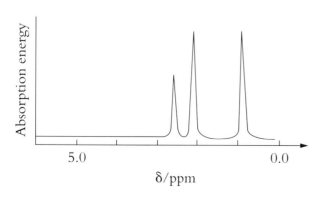

Type of proton	Chemical shift/ ppm
$R{-}CH_3$	0.9
$R{-}CH_2{-}R$	1.3
R_3CH	2.0
$R{-}CO{-}CH_3$	2.1
$R{-}CH_2{-}CO{-}R$	2.5
$R{-}CH{=}CH_2$	4.7–5.9
$R{-}CHO$	9.7

MULTIPLE COMPLETION QUESTIONS

Questions 17–30 are multiple completion items. For each multiple completion question ONE or MORE of the responses given is/are correct. Decide which of the responses is/are correct. Then refer to the table to select your answer A, B, C or D.

Summarised directions for multiple completion questions			
A (i), (ii) and (iii) only	**B** (i) and (iii) only	**C** (ii) and (iv) only	**D** (iv) only

17 In which of these molecules do all the atoms lie in the same plane?

  (i) C_6H_6

  (ii) HCHO

  (iii) $C_2H_2Cl_2$

  (iv) CH_3CO_2H

18 Which of these compounds are structural isomers of heptane?

  (i)   2,3-dimethylpentane

  (ii) 2,2,3-trimethylbutane

  (iii) 3-ethylpentane

  (iv) 2,2,3,3-tetramethylbutane

19 In which of these compounds is there hydrogen bonding between the molecules?

  (i) CH_3CH_2OH

  (ii) CH_2Cl_2

  (iii) $CH_3CH_2NH_2$

  (iv) $CH_3CO_2CH_2CH_3$

20 These statements describe potassium bromide. Which of the statements is/are also true of 1-bromobutane?

  (i)   a crystalline solid at room temperature

  (ii) soluble in water

  (iii) an electrical conductor when liquid

  (iv) a colourless compound

Summarised directions for multiple completion questions			
A (i), (ii) and (iii) only	**B** (i) and (iii) only	**C** (ii) and (iv) only	**D** (iv) only

21 Which of these compounds has/have geometric isomers?

(i) but-1-ene

(ii) but-2-ene

(iii) 2-methylbut-2-ene

(iv) 1,2-dichloroethene

22 Which of these molecules is/are chiral?

(i) 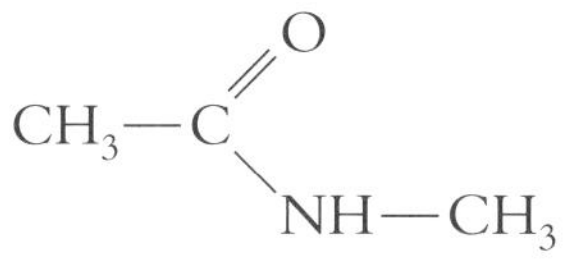 CH_3—C $\overset{\displaystyle O}{\underset{\displaystyle NH—CH_3}{}}$

(ii) 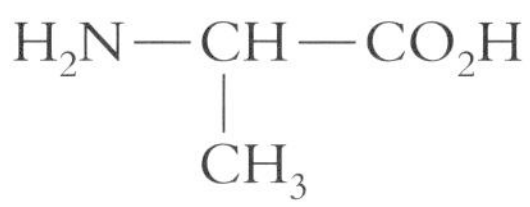 H_2N—CH—CO_2H with CH_3

(iii) 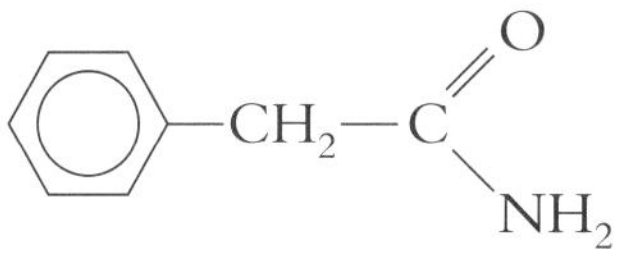   ⬡—CH_2—C $\overset{\displaystyle O}{\underset{\displaystyle NH_2}{}}$

(iv) 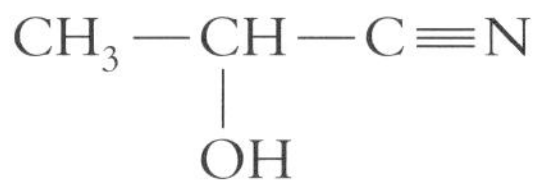 CH_3—CH—$C≡N$ with OH

23 In which of these reactions are the intermediates free radicals?

(i) ethane with chlorine in UV light

(ii) thermal cracking of hydrocarbons

(iii) polymerisation of phenylethene in the presence of benzoyl peroxide

(iv) catalytic cracking of hydrocarbons

Summarised directions for multiple completion questions			
A (i), (ii) and (iii) only	**B** (i) and (iii) only	**C** (ii) and (iv) only	**D** (iv) only

24 Oxidation of $C_4H_{10}O$ gave a ketone C_4H_8O as the product. Possible starting materials are:
(i) $(CH_3)_3COH$
(ii) $CH_3CH_2CH_2CH_2OH$
(iii) $(CH_3)_2CHCH_2OH$
(iv) $CH_3CH_2CH(OH)CH_3$

25 Which of these liquids react readily with PCl_5, giving off a gas which fumes in moist air?
(i) CH_3CH_2OH
(ii) CH_3COCH_3
(iii) CH_3CO_2H
(iv) $CH_3CO_2C_2H_5$

26 Which of these reactions produce butylamine?
(i) Heating butanamide with P_2O_5
(ii) Heating 1-bromobutane with concentrated ammonia under pressure
(iii) Heating N-methyl butanamide with aqueous sodium hydroxide
(iv) Reducing propanenitrile with $LiAlH_4$

27 Which of these compounds are hydrolysed to give sodium propanoate as one of the products when heated under reflux with aqueous sodium hydroxide?
(i) CH_3CH_2CN
(ii) CH_3CONH_2
(iii) $CH_3CH_2CO_2CH_2CH_3$
(iv) $CH_3CH_2CH_2COCH_3$

28 Which reagents are used to acylate primary amines?
(i) sodium ethanoate
(ii) ethanoic anhydride
(iii) ethanoic acid
(iv) ethanoyl chloride

Summarised directions for multiple completion questions			
A	**B**	**C**	**D**
(i), (ii) and (iii) only	(i) and (iii) only	(ii) and (iv) only	(iv) only

29 As a result of delocalisation of electrons:

    (i)   benzene undergoes substitution rather than addition reactions

    (ii)   ethanoic acid is a stronger acid than ethanol

    (iii) phenylamine is a weaker base than ethylamine

    (iv) ethylamine is a stronger base than ammonia.

30 Which of these are examples of condensation polymers?

(i)

$$-\overset{\displaystyle H}{\underset{\displaystyle H}{C}}-\overset{\displaystyle CH_3}{\underset{\displaystyle CO_2CH_3}{C}}-\overset{\displaystyle H}{\underset{\displaystyle H}{C}}-\overset{\displaystyle CH_3}{\underset{\displaystyle CO_2CH_3}{C}}-$$

(ii)

$$-\overset{O}{\overset{\|}{C}}-\bigcirc-\overset{O}{\overset{\|}{C}}-O-CH_2-CH_2-O-\overset{O}{\overset{\|}{C}}-\bigcirc-\overset{O}{\overset{\|}{C}}-O-CH_2-CH_2-O-$$

(iii)

$$-\overset{F}{\underset{F}{C}}-\overset{F}{\underset{F}{C}}-\overset{F}{\underset{F}{C}}-\overset{F}{\underset{F}{C}}-\overset{F}{\underset{F}{C}}-\overset{F}{\underset{F}{C}}-$$

(iv)

$$-\overset{O}{\overset{\|}{C}}-(CH_2)_4-\overset{O}{\overset{\|}{C}}-\underset{H}{N}-(CH_2)_6-\underset{H}{N}-\overset{O}{\overset{\|}{C}}-(CH_2)_4-\overset{O}{\overset{\|}{C}}-\underset{H}{N}-(CH_2)_6-NH-$$

A-Z Answers

Note that these answers are kept concise, while giving as much helpful information as possible. Sometimes, the answers give you enough information to check your responses, while not giving all the information you are asked for. For example, the answers often show the structural formulae of organic compounds rather than the displayed formulae.

Acid–base titrations

Missing information in order: 82, 82, 0.50, 0.50, 0.50, 0.010, 0.025, 0.020, 1, 2, 2, Na_2HPO_3, 2.

Answers: 138 g mol^{-1}, 39 g mol^{-1}

Acids

Missing information in order: 7, indicators, 2, $MgCl_2$, carbonates, calcium carbonate, $CaCO_3$, metal (or basic), $MgSO_4$, $H_2O(l)$.

They all contain hydrogen, $H^+(aq)$ ions or oxonium ionds, $H_3O^+(aq)$.

Strong: hydrochloric, nitric and sulfuric acids.

Weak: chloric(I), ethanoic and sulfurous acids.

Activation energy

1 True   5 False
2 True   6 True
3 False   7 True
4 False

Missing words in order: temperature, temperature, collide, activation, doubles.

Acyl chlorides

a $CH_3CO-OC_2H_5$
b ethyl ethanoate,
c C_2H_5OH
d ammonia, NH_3
e ethanamide
f $CH_3CO-NHC_2H_5$
g N-ethyl ethanamide,

Missing word: rapid/fast

Addition–elimination reactions

First step: addition
Second step: gain and loss of protons
Third step: elimination
Product: ethyl ethanoate

Addition polymers

a ethene

b poly(ethene) or polythene

c

d poly(phenylethene) or polystyrene

e

f

g tetrafluoroethene

h poly(tetrafluoroethene) or PTFE

Addition reactions

Missing words in order: two, single, unsaturated, alkenes, 1,2-dibromoethane.

Air pollution

Acid rain.

The greenhouse effect.

Formation of ozone in the lower atmosphere and photochemical smog.

Thinning of the ozone layer in the upper atmosphere.

Alcohols

1	D	7	B
2	F	8	I
3	E	9	H
4	C	10	N
5	J	11	M
6	K	12	G

Aldehydes

1	Propanal	7	Propanoic
2	Reducing	8	Fehlings
3	Hydrogen cyanide	9	Addition
4	Tollens	10	Polar
5	Green	11	Recrystallise
6	Orange		

Reading down the grid: nucleophile.

Alkanes

Names: 2-methylpropane, 2,4-dimethylpentane

Labelling: C_4H_{10}, melting and boiling points increase, increasing chain length, area of contact between molecules increases, $C_{10}H_{22}$

Reactions: **a** chloroethane, **b** chlorine, **c** substitution, **d** UV light, **e** substitution, **f** bromoethane, **g** CH_3CH_2Br, **h** combustion, **i** cracking, **j** $CH_2=CH_2$, **k** ethene.

Alkenes

Names: propene, but-2-ene, but-1-ene.

Bonds: C—C and C—H are sigma (σ) bonds, the charge clouds make up a pi (π) bond.

Property 1: no rotation about the double bond so bringing about the existence of geometric isomers.

Property 2: Tendency to undergo addition reactions.

Reactions: **a** ethane, **b** hydrogen with a platinum catalyst, **c** 1,2-dibromoethane, **d** bromine at room temperature, **e** CH_3—CH_2Br, **f** absorb in concentrated sulfuric acid at room temperature, **g** CH_3—CH_2OH, **h** ethanol.

Aluminium extraction

a Carbon anode
b Molten electrolyte
c Molten aluminium
d Carbon cathode
Anode: $2O^{2-} \rightarrow O_2 + 4e^-$
Cathode: $Al^{3+} + 3e^- \rightarrow Al$

1 The electrolyte must be molten so that the ions can move to the electrodes. Aluminium oxide has a very high melting point. The mixture of the oxide with sodium hexafluoroalumiante(III) (cryolite) melts at a much lower temperature.

2 The oxygen given off at the anodes reacts with the hot carbon. So, the anodes burn away.

Amides

1 Propanamide: CH_3CONH_2
2 Ethylamine: $CH_3CH_2NH_2$
3 Ethanenitrile: CH_3CN
4 Propylamine: $CH_3CH_2NH_2$

Amines

ALKYL AMINES

1 $CH_3CH_2CH_2CH_2NH_3^+Cl^-$
2 Nucleophilic substitution
3 ethylamine, diethylamine, triethylamine and the quaternary ammonium salt, $(C_2H_5)_4N^+Br^-$

ARYL AMINES

a benzene
b mixture of concentrated nitric and sulfuric acids at room temperature
c nitrobenzene, C_6H_5—NO_2
d phenylamine

BASE STRENGTH

propylamine > ammonia > phenylamine

In propylamine the inductive effect of the alkyl group releases electrons to increase the electron density on the nitrogen atom, so it can hold onto an extra proton more strongly.

In phenylamine the lone pair of electrons on the N atom is less available for bonding with a proton because it links up with the system of delocalised electrons in the benzene ring.

Amino acids

1 Glycine: H_2N—CH_2—CO_2H
Alanine: H_2N—$CHCH_3$—CO_2H
2 There are four different groups round the central C atom in alanine. An alanine molecule is chiral. Glycine with two hydrogen atoms attached to the central C atom has a plane of symmetry and is not chiral.

3 H_3N^+—$CHCH_3$—CO_2^-

4　**a**　H_3N^+—$CHCH_3$—CO_2H

　　b　H_2N—$CHCH_3$—CO_2^-

5　Peptide group shown in bold:

　　H_2N—$CHCH_3$—**CO**—**HN**—CH_2—CO_2H

　　H_2N—CH_2—**CO**—**HN**—$CHCH_3$—CO_2H

Ammonia manufacture

Sequence: **D–B–C–A**

Effect of pressure: **F–C–G–H–A**

Effect of temperature: **F–D–E–B**

Amounts of chemicals

Missing information in order: atoms, 12.00 g, mol, g, $g\ mol^{-1}$.

1　**a**　0.05 mol

　　b　0.25 mol

　　c　0.025 mol

2　**a**　328 g

　　b　0.85 g

　　c　0.04 g

3　**a**　4 mol

　　b　2 mol

　　c　1.0 mol

　　d　0.2 mol

4　0.04 mol

Aromatic hydrocarbons (arenes)

Names and structures: methyl benzene,

, naphthalene

1　All the C—C bonds in benzene are the same length/strength

2　The benzene molecule is planar

3　Benzene is more stable than might otherwise be expected

4　The characteristic reactions are substitution rather than addition reactions

5　The reagents that attack benzene are electrophiles.

Chlorination: chlorobenzene

Nitration: nitrobenzene

Alkylation: methylbenzene

Acylation: phenylethanone

Arrhenius equation

1　k: rate constant

　　E_a: activation energy

　　R: gas constant

　　T: temperature in Kelvins

2　Measure the rate, and hence the rate constant, at a series of temperatures.

Plot a graph of ln k against $1/T$.

Measure the gradient of the graph and calculate the activation energy given that the gradient = $-E_a/RT$.

Avogadro constant

1　1.20×10^{22} atoms

2　1.20×10^{22} molecules

3　6.02×10^{23} atoms

4　6.02×10^{24} molecules

5　9.03×10^{23} ions

Balanced equations

1　$C_2H_4(g) + 3O_2(g) \rightarrow 2CO_2(g) + 2H_2O(l)$

2　$4NH_3(g) + 5O_2(g) \rightarrow 4NO(g) + 6H_2O(g)$

3　$2Na(s) + 2H_2O(l) \rightarrow 2NaOH(aq) + H_2(g)$

4　$Cl_2(g) + H_2O(l) \rightarrow HOCl(aq) + HCl(aq)$

Benzene

1　The benzene molecule is a regular hexagon with all the bonds the same length/strength.

There are no isomers of 1,2-dichlorobenzene.

The characteristic reactions of benzene are substitution reactions and not addition reactions.

2　6

3　The enthalpy change on hydrogenating 1 mol benzene is about 150 kJ less negative (so less exothermic) than the enthalpy change for hydrogenating three normal double bonds.

Bond breaking

1　Homolytic

2　Heterolytic

3　Heterolytic

4　Heterolytic

5　Homolytic

6　Homolytic

7　Heterolytic

8　Homolytic

The bond which breaks in the ester is the C—O bond and not the O—C_2H_5 bond.

Bond enthalpies

1　$\Delta H = -186\ kJ\ mol^{-1}$

2　$\Delta H = -170\ kJ\ mol^{-1}$

3　$\Delta H = -81\ kJ\ mol^{-1}$

4　$\Delta H = -730\ kJ\ mol^{-1}$

Bond lengths

Order of bond lengths: $C—C > C=C > C\equiv C$

In benzene all the bond lengths are the same: and intermediate between $C—C$ and $C=C$.

Born–Haber cycle

1 D
2 C
3 A
4 B

ΔH_1 = standard enthalpy change of formation of calcium chloride
ΔH_2 = enthalpy of atomisation of calcium
ΔH_3 = first ionisation energy of calcium
ΔH_4 = second ionisation energy of calcium
ΔH_5 = twice the enthalpy change of atomisation of chlorine
ΔH_6 = twice the electron affinity of chlorine

Lattice enthalpy, $\Delta H_7 = -2253$ kJ mol^{-1}

Bromine extraction

1 D
2 C
3 B
4 A

Stage 1: $Cl_2 + 2Br^- \rightarrow 2Cl^- + Br_2$
Stage 3: $Br_2(g) + SO_2(g) + 2H_2O(l) \rightarrow$
$\quad\quad\quad\quad\quad 4H^+(aq) + 2Br^-(aq) + SO_4^{2-}(aq)$
Stage 4: $Cl_2 + 2Br^- \rightarrow 2Cl^- + Br_2$

Uses: to make flame retardants, agricultural chemicals, synthetic rubber for the inner lining of tubeless tyres, dyes and a range of chemical intermediates.

Brønsted–Lowry theory

1 i
2 e
3 e, f
4 a, d, e, f, g, k
5 b, c, d, h, j
6 d
7 a, k
8 g
9 c
10 f
11 a, g
12 d, k
13 b, j
14 h

Buffer solutions

A 7
B 3
C 2
D 8
E 5
F 1
G 6
H 4

pH = 5.1

Carbonyl compounds

Missing terms in order: C=O/carbonyl, aldehydes, ketones, polar, electronegative, nucleophilic, addition.

Carboxylic acids

a C_2H_5OH
b PCl_5
c $LiAlH_4$
d $CH_3CO—OC_2H_5$
e sodium ethanoate
f ester
g acyl chloride
h ethanol

Catalysts

A 3
B 5
C 1
D 4
E 2

First graph: vertical axis – energy, horizontal axis – progress/extent of reaction, upper left horizontal line – reactants, lower right horizontal line – products, longer arrow – activation energy without catalyst, shorter arrow – activation energy with catalyst.

Second graph: vertical axis – number of molecules with kinetic energy E, horizontal axis – kinetic energy E, energy corresponding to left-hand dotted line – activation energy with catalyst, energy corresponding to right-hand dotted line – activation energy without catalyst, area under curve to the right of the right-hand dotted line – number of molecules able to react without catalyst, area under curve to the right of the left-hand dotted line – number of molecules able to react with catalyst.

Catalytic converter

a carbon monoxide, CO
b nitrogen oxides, NO_x
c unburnt fuel

Gases leaving converter: N_2, H_2O and CO_2.

Changes of state

Boxes in order: solid, liquid, gas

a melting (endothermic)
b vaporising/evaporation (endothermic)
c freezing (exothermic)
d condensing (exothermic)

Solid: particles packed close together and vibrating about fixed positions.

Liquid: particles close together but free to move about sliding past each other.

Gas: particles spread out, moving fast and colliding with each other and the walls of the container.

Chelates

Missing letters: A, R, P, S, I, C, D, S, T, N, D, E, L, O, D, A, R, T (Full stop between N and C) H, E, F, Y, N, A, D, T, A, U, H. T (full-stop between A and C) L, A, E , L, R, B, C, E, I, D, T, A.

Chiral compounds

Chiral centre marked with an asterisk:

A

$$CH_3—\overset{\overset{\textstyle OH}{|}}{\underset{\underset{\textstyle H}{|}}{C^*}}—CO_2H$$

C

$$H_2N—\overset{\overset{\textstyle OH}{|}}{\underset{\underset{\textstyle H}{|}}{C^*}}—CO_2H$$

D

$$C_2H_5—\overset{\overset{\textstyle H}{|}}{\underset{\underset{\textstyle CH_3}{|}}{C^*}}—C_4H_9$$

Mirror images:

Main difference: the two mirror image forms are optical isomers. They rotate the plane of polarised light in opposite directions.

Living things: chirality is very important because living cells are full of messenger, carrier molecules which interact selectively with the active sites and receptors in other molecules such as enzymes. The messenger and carrier molecules are all chiral and the body works with only one of the mirror image forms. In most living things all the amino acids, for example, are L-amino acids.

Chlorine

a $Fe^{3+}(aq) + Cl^-(aq)$
b Al(s), heat
c Burn $H_2(g)$ in chlorine
d $CH_3Cl(g)$ and HCl(g) plus further substitution products (CH_2Cl_2, $CHCl_3$, CCl_4)
e $Br_2(aq)$ and chloride ions
f Hot NaOH(aq)
g NaOH(aq) at room temperature
h HOCl(aq) + HCl(aq)

Complex ions

1	B	7	H
2	E	8	B, D
3	C	9	A, C, J (also G, H)
4	D, E, H, I, J	10	C
5	A	11	F
6	G	12	D

Concentrations

1 0.04 mol dm^{-3}
2 1.00 mol dm^{-3}
3 $0.125 \text{ mol dm}^{-3}$
4 1.00 mol dm^{-3}
5 $0.0125 \text{ mol dm}^{-3}$
6 $0.00005 \text{ mol dm}^{-3}$

Condensation polymerisation

Missing words in order: molecule, water/hydrogen chloride, ester, monomers, chains, polyamides, polyesters, strong, polar.

Corrosion

1 Fe and $Fe(OH)_2$
2 O_2
3 $Fe_2O_3.nH_2O(s)$
4 Where Fe is oxidised to Fe^{2+}
5 Where electrons are supplied to reduce O_2.

Covalent bonding

Covalent giant structures

Two examples such as: diamond, graphite, silicon dioxide

a Hard and strong
b Normally non-conductors of electricity
c The network of strong covalent bonding is continuous with no weak links
d Graphite
e Solvent cannot bond strongly enough with non-metal atoms to break up the giant structure

Covalent molecular structures

Elements with covalently bonded molecules: all halogens, oxygen, sulfur, nitrogen, hydrogen.

Compounds with covalently bonded molecules: most compounds of metal with non-metals such as the hydrides of oxygen, nitrogen and the halogens; the oxides of carbon, nitrogen, sulfur and phosphorus; the chlorides of carbon, silicon, phosphorus and sulfur; also most organic compounds.

a Low melting and boiling points
b Insoluble in water but soluble in organic solvents
c Molecules are uncharged. There are no free electrons.

d Molecules such as alcohols and amines with electronegative oxygen or nitrogen atoms can form hydrogen bonds with water.

Dative covalent bonds

Delocalisation of electrons

1 ✔	6 ✔
2 ✔	7 ✔
3 ✗	8 ✗
4 ✗	9 ✔
5 ✗	10 ✔

Diazonium salts

A	5	**E**	6
B	1	**F**	3
C	8	**G**	4
D	2	**H**	7

Disproportionation

1 Chlorine disproportionates:
$Cl(0) \rightarrow Cl(+1) + Cl(-1)$
2 Not disproportionation.
3 Oxygen disproportionates: $O(-1) \rightarrow O(-2) + O(0)$

Electrochemical cells

a Hydrogen gas at 100 kPa pressure (1 atmosphere) and 298 K
b Platinum electrode covered with platinum black
c 1.0 mol dm^{-3} $H^+(aq)$ at 298 K
d Salt bridge
e High resistance voltmeter
f Zinc electrode
g 1.0 mol dm^{-3} $Zn^+(aq)$ at 298 K

1 By definition, if the left-hand electrode is a standard hydrogen electrode, the cell emf is the standard electrode potential of the right-hand electrode.
  a -0.40 V
  b $+0.80 \text{ V}$
  c $+1.09 \text{ V}$

2 **a** $+1.20 \text{ V}$
  b $+0.29 \text{ V}$
  c -1.49 V
3 $Cd(s) + 2Ag^+(aq) \rightarrow Cd^{2+}(aq) + 2Ag(s)$
  $2Ag(s) + Br_2(aq) \rightarrow 2Ag^+(aq) + 2Br^-(aq)$
  $Cd(s) + Br_2(aq) \rightarrow Cd^{2+}(aq) + 2Br^-(aq)$

Electrode potentials

1 Magnesium metal
2 Aqueous chlorine
3 **a** $2Fe^{3+}(aq) + 2I^-(aq) \rightarrow 2Fe^{2+}(aq) + I_2(aq)$
  b $Mg(s) + Cu^{2+}(aq) \rightarrow Mg^{2+}(aq) + Cu(s)$
  c No reaction
  d $Fe^{3+}(aq) + Fe(s) \rightarrow 2Fe^{2+}(aq)$
  e $2V^{3+}(aq) + Zn(s) \rightarrow 2V^{2+}(aq) + Zn^{2+}(s)$
  f No reaction

Electrolysis of brine

a Sodium chloride solution (brine), $NaCl(aq)$
b Chlorine gas, $Cl_2(g)$
c Hydrogen gas, $H_2(g)$
d Sodium hydroxide solution, $NaOH(aq)$

1 Anode: $2Cl^-(aq) \rightarrow Cl_2(g) + 2e^-$
  Cathode: $2H^+(aq) + 2e^- \rightarrow H_2(g)$
2 Chlorine: water purification, manufacture of hydrochloric acid, also to make organic compounds such as the polymer PVC, and to make bleach.

  Sodium hydroxide: used to make soap from fats and oils, used to purify bauxite for aluminium manufacture, used as an alkali in the manufacture of a wide range of chemicals

  Hydrogen: used to manufacture ammonia and methanol, also to hydrogenate unsaturated vegetable oils.

Electron configurations

Missing words in order: lowest, two, energy level, spins.

N: 1s ⇅ 2s ⇅ 2p ↑ ↑ ↑
Na: 1s ⇅ 2s ⇅ 2p ⇅ ⇅ ⇅ 3s ↑
S: 1s ⇅ 2s ⇅ 2p ⇅ ⇅ ⇅ 3s ⇅ 3p ⇅ ↑ ↑

Potassium: $1s^2 2s^2 2p^6 3s^2 3p^6 4s^1$
Magnesium: $1s^2 2s^2 2p^6 3s^2$
Fluorine: $1s^2 2s^2 2p^5$
Chlorine: $1s^2 2s^2 2p^6 3s^2 3p^5$

Electrophilic addition

1 alkenes
2 chlorine, bromine, hydrogen bromide, sulfuric acid
3 heterolytic
4 the movement of a pair of electrons
5 ion, positive

Electrophilic substitution

1

Br
| ⁻
Br—Fe—Br   Br⁺
|
Br

2 Br^+
3 The metal atom in both compounds is an electron pair acceptor (a Lewis acid).

4 a

b Addition would lead to a diene, which would not be stabilised by delocalisation. Loss of a proton restores the ring of delocalised electrons, which stabilises the benzene ring.

Empirical formula

Missing numbers.
Combining masses: 51.6 g
Molar masses: 12.0, 16.0
Amounts: $38.7 \text{ g}/12.0 \text{ g mol}^{-1} = 3.22 \text{ mol}$,
$9.7 \text{ g}/1.0 \text{ g mol}^{-1} = 9.7 \text{ mol}$,
$51.6 \text{ g}/16.0 \text{ g mol}^{-1} = 3.23 \text{ mol}$
Simplest ratio: 1:3:1
Formula: CH_3O

a $CuCl$
b PbN_2O_6
c $C_2H_5NO_2$

Enthalpy changes

1 D
2 A
3 E
4 B
5 C

Standard conditions for thermochemistry: 298 K, 100 kPa (1 atmosphere pressure).

Enthalpy change of formation

a: $2C(s) + 2H_2(g) + 3O_2(g)$
b: $C_2H_4(g) + 3O_2(g)$
c: $2CO_2(g) + 2H_2O(l)$

$\Delta H_2^{\ominus} = -1360 \text{ kJ mol}^{-1}$
$\Delta H_3^{\ominus} = -1411 \text{ kJ mol}^{-1}$
$\Delta H_f^{\ominus}[C_2H_4] = +51 \text{ kJ mol}^{-1}$

Enthalpy change of reaction

a: $C_2H_4(g) + H_2O(g)$
b: $C_2H_5OH(l)$
c: $2C(s) + 3H_2(g) + \frac{1}{2}O_2(g)$

$\Delta H_2^{\ominus} = -191 \text{ kJ mol}^{-1}$
$\Delta H_3^{\ominus} = -277 \text{ kJ mol}^{-1}$
$\Delta H_1^{\ominus} = -86 \text{ kJ mol}^{-1}$

Enthalpy change of solution

Missing words in order: 1 mol, standard, difference, hydrated

a $NaCl(s)$
b $Na^+(g)$
c $Cl^-(g)$

$NaCl(s) + aq \rightarrow Na^+(aq) + Cl^-(aq)$
$$\Delta H_{solution}^{\ominus} = +4 \text{ kJ mol}^{-1}$$

Missing words in order: large, greater, hydrated.

Entropy

1 D   4 A
2 F   5 C
3 B   6 E

Enzymes

Missing words in order: protein, catalysts, hydrolysis, reaction, temperature, pH.

Esters

In each case the ester link is:

O   O
|| ||
—O—C—   or   —C—O—

A Fruit flavour
B Aspirin
C Fat
D Polyester

1 Acid catalysed reversible.
   Products: $CH_3CO_2H + C_2H_5OH$
2 Base catalysed not reversible.
   Products: $CH_3CO_2^- + C_2H_5OH$

Ethene

a Chlorine
b Ethanol
c Poly(ethene)
d A plastic for wrapping film, plastic bags, bowls and bottles.

e A plastic used for pipes, guttering and window frames, bottles, films and sheets.

f A plastic used for a variety of containers and, when expanded, for insulation and packaging.

Eutrophication

5–1–6–2–4–3

Fractional distillation of oil

Gas: Gaseous fuels including bottled gas

Gasoline: Blended to make petrol

Naphtha: Cracked thermally to make ethene and other chemicals

Kerosine: Aviation fuel

Gas oil: Diesel fuel for trucks, cars, trains and ships

Heavy gas oil: Fuel for ships and power stations

Lubricating oil: Lubricating machinery

Catalytic cracker feed: Cracked to make lighter fractions for petrol

Residue: tar for roads and roofs

1 Methane, CH_4; ethane, C_2H_6; propane, C_3H_8; butane, C_4H_{10}.

2

3 To provide ingredients for making petrol, since there is not enough of the gasoline fraction to meet demand for motor fuel.

To make ethene and other alkenes, which are the starting points for synthesis in the petrochemical industry.

Free energy

1 ΔG must be negative

2 $\Delta G = \Delta H - T\Delta S$

3 At about room temperature for many reactions, $\Delta G \approx \Delta H$. Values of ΔH are easier to obtain and data on the entropy change may not be available.

4 a $\Delta H^{\ominus} = -171.2 \text{ kJ mol}^{-1}$

b $\Delta S^{\ominus} = -322.2 \text{ J mol}^{-1} \text{ K}^{-1}$
($= -0.322 \text{ kJ mol}^{-1} \text{ K}^{-1}$)

c At 1000 K, $\Delta G = +150.8 \text{ kJ mol}^{-1}$

d At 298 K: spontaneous (does tend to go)
At 1000 K: not spontaneous (does not tend to go).

Free radical reactions

a Initiation

b Termination

c The steps that produce the products

d The steps that remove free radicals from the reaction mixture

e $Cl—Cl \rightarrow Cl\bullet + Cl\bullet$

f $CH_4 + Cl\bullet \rightarrow CH_3\bullet + HCl$
$CH_3\bullet + Cl_2 \rightarrow CH_3Cl + Cl\bullet$

If chlorine is in excess, further substitution leads to the formation of CH_2Cl_2, $CHCl_3$ and CCl_4.

Friedel–Crafts reaction

1 It is a way of creating C—C bonds and building up the carbon skeleton of a molecule during synthesis.

2 $AlCl_3$. The aluminium atom in this compound is an electron pair acceptor (a Lewis acid).

3

Fuels

1	Reforming	**7**	Gasohol
2	Biofuel	**8**	Energy density
3	Petrol	**9**	Octane number
4	Ethanol	**10**	Cracking
5	Hydrocarbon	**11**	Knocking
6	Diesel	**12**	Fossil

Functional groups (AS)

1 F, 2,2-dimethylpropan-1-ol

2 C, pentanal

3 D, but-2-ene

4 H, 2-bromopentane

5 G, butanoic acid

6 B, 2-chloro-2-methylpropane

7 I, 1-iodohexane

8 J, butanone

9 A, butan-2-ol

10 E, 2-methylbutan-2-ol

Functional groups (A2)

1 G, ethanoic anhydride

2 C, ethanoyl chloride

3 A, propanamide

4 H, alanine (2-aminopropanoic acid)

5 D, methylbenzene (toluene)

6 J, ethyl propanoate

7 F, propanenitrile

8 B, nitrobenzene

9 K, phenol

10 I, ethylamine

11 E, phenylamine

Fundamental particles

a 1   c +1
b −1   d 0

Gas tests

1 Hydrogen
2 Nitrogen dioxide, oxygen
3 Oxygen
4 Hydrogen chloride
5 Carbon dioxide
6 Ammonia
7 Chlorine
8 Sulfur dioxide
9 Water vapour
10 Hydrogen sulfide

Gas volume calculations

Missing words in order: equal, equal, one mole, temperature, pressure.

1 Hydrogen bromide, 20 cm^3
2 C_6H_{12}
3 701 cm^3 (0.70 dm^3)

Geometric isomerism

Trans but-2-ene   *Cis* but-2-ene

Giant structures

A Ionic bonding, sodium chloride
B Covalent bonding, silicon dioxide
C Metallic bonding, examples of hexagonal close-packing: magnesium, scandium, titanium, zinc, cadmium and some less common metals

Grignard reagents

a CO_2 (carbon dioxide)
b Hydrocarbon

c

d

Group 1

1 True
2 True
3 False (the atoms lose the one electron in the outer shell to form smaller ions).
4 False (it is the anions in some group 1 metal compounds which make a solution alkaline not the cations).
5 True
6 False (a sodium flame is bright yellow).
7 True
8 False (sodium, for example, forms a mixture of oxides: Na_2O and Na_2O_2).
9 True
10 True
11 False (Li_2CO_3 decomposes on heating).
12 False (sodium and potassium carbonates, for example, are soluble, though lithium carbonate is sparingly soluble).
13 False ($LiNO_3$ behaves like a group 2 nitrate and decomposes to the oxide, oxygen and nitrogen dioxide; the statement is true for true of $NaNO_3$ and KNO_3).
14 False (all group 1 hydroxides are soluble and solubility increases down the group).
15 True

Group 2

1 $2Mg(s) + O_2(g) \rightarrow 2MgO(s)$
2 $Mg(s) + Cl_2(g) \rightarrow MgCl_2(s)$
3 $Mg(s) + H_2O(g) \rightarrow MgO(s) + H_2(g)$
4 $Ca(s) + 2H_2O(l) \rightarrow Ca(OH)_2(s) + H_2(g)$
5 $BaO(s) + 2HNO_3(aq) \rightarrow Ba(NO_3)_2(aq) + H_2O(l)$
6 $Ca(OH)_2(s) + 2HCl(aq) \rightarrow CaCl_2(aq) + 2H_2O(l)$
7 $MgCO_3(s) \rightarrow MgO(s) + CO_2(g)$
8 $Ba^{2+}(aq) + SO_4{}^{2-}(aq) \rightarrow BaSO_4(s)$
A Increase
B Decrease
C Increase
D Increase
E Increase
F Decrease

Group 4

1	a = 2	7	g = +4
2	b = 2	8	h = +2
3	c = 4	9	i = +4
4	d = 3	10	j = +4
5	e = 60	11	k = +2
6	f = +2	12	l = +2

Atomic number of Ge = 32
Hardness of diamond = 10

Percentage of tin in bronze = 20%
Melting point of silicon = 1410 °C
Transition temperature for Sn = 13.2 °C

Halides
Missing words in order: colourless, fume, very soluble, acidic, strong, ionise.

Oxidation states:
$+6 – H_2SO_4$
$+4 – SO_2$
$-2 – H_2S$
$I^- > Br^- > Cl^-$

a white
b readily
c $AgBr$
d concentrated
e silver bromide
f not

Halogenoalkanes
A 2-methylpropanenitrile, $CH_3CHCNCH_3$
B Propan-2-ol, $CH_3CHOHCH_3$
C Heat with ammonia in ethanol
D Heat with a concentrated solution of KOH in ethanol
E Pass vapour over hot aluminium oxide or heat with concentrated phosphoric acid or heat with excess concentrated sulfuric acid.
F 2-aminopropane
G propene

Halogens are useful intermediates. Their substitution and elimination reactions allow the synthesis of a wide range of compounds.

Halogens
A Chlorine
B Astatine
C Fluorine
D Iodine
E Group seven
F Halides
G Bromine
H Salt former

Fluorine: PTFE
Chlorine: Bleaching
Bromine: Photographs
Iodine: Pharmaceuticals

Hess's law
$\Delta H_1 = \Delta H_2 + \Delta H_3 + \Delta H_4$

The law states that the enthalpy change for a reaction is the same whether it takes place in one step or a series of steps. So long as the reactants and the products are the same, the overall enthalpy change will be the same.

Heterogeneous catalysis
Iron: **B** (manufacture of ammonia used to make nitric acid, nylon, fertilisers, explosives and dyes)

Nickel: **A** (hardening to vegetable oils in the manufacture of margarine)

Platinum/rhodium: **E** (step during the manufacture of nitric acid from ammonia), **G** (removal of pollutant gases from motor vehicle exhausts)

Silver: **D** (product used to make antifreeze, solvents and surfactants)

Vanadium(v) oxide: **C** (step in the manufacture of sulfuric acid)

Zeolite: **F** (catalytic cracking to increase the yield of useful small molecules from crude oil)

Heterogeneous equilibrium
1 $CaCO_3(s) \rightarrow CaO(s) + CO_2(g)$
2 At a constant temperature in a closed container (so that the gas cannot escape).
3 $K_c = [CO_2(g)]$
4 $K_p = p_{CO_2}$

Homogeneous catalysis
Missing words in order: phase, catalyst, solvent.

$Fe^{3+}(aq)$: **B**
$H^+(aq)$: **C**
$Mn^{2+}(aq)$ **A**

Homogeneous equilibrium
1 $CH_3CO—OC_2H_5(l) + H_2O(l) \rightleftharpoons$
$$CH_3CO_2H(l) + C_2H_5OH(l)$$
2 At constant temperature in a closed system.

3
$$K_c = \frac{[CH_3CO_2H(l)][C_2H_5OH(l)]}{[CH_3CO—OC_2H_5(l)][H_2O(l)]}$$

Ideal and real gases
p: N m^{-2} (Pa)
V: m^3
n: mol
R: J K^{-1} mol^{-1}
T: K

Close to ideal: argon, helium, hydrogen, nitrogen, oxygen
Not ideal: ammonia, carbon dioxide, chlorine

Infrared spectroscopy
A 2
B 3
C 1
D 4

Initial rate method
a 0.00576
b 0.003
c 0.00192
d 0.003

From experiment 1: $k = 80\ 000\ mol^{-2}\ dm^6\ s^{-1}$

Intermediate bonding
a KF, BaO
b $AlCl_3$, MgI_2
c HBr
d Br_2, O_2

Intermediates in reactions
1 Free radicals: $Cl\bullet$ and $CH_3\bullet$.
2 Carbocation: $CH_3\!\!-\!\!CH_2^+$
3 Carbocation: $(CH_3)_3C^+$
4 Cation:

Intermolecular forces
Temporary dipole – temporary dipole:
CH_4, Cl_2, C_3H_8

Permanent dipole – permanent dipole: HBr, CH_3Cl, HCHO

Hydrogen bonding: NH_3, HF, C_2H_5OH, H_2O

Ionic bonding

K^+ $:\!\overset{\times\times}{\underset{\times\times}{F}}\!:^-$ Mg^{2+} $:\!\overset{\times\times}{\underset{\times\times}{O}}\!:^{2-}$ $\overset{\times\times}{\underset{\times\times}{C}}\!:^-$ Ca^{2+} $\overset{\times\times}{\underset{\times\times}{C}}\!:^-$

a Strong electrostatic attraction throughout the crystals
b Non-conductors when solid but conduct when molten
c Soluble in water (but not in non-polar solvents)
d If layers of ions slip then ions with the same charge come up against each other – like charges repel and break up the crystals.

Ionic product of water
1 $2H_2O(l) \rightleftharpoons H_3O^+(aq) + OH^-(aq)$ or
   $H_2O(l) \rightleftharpoons H^+(aq) + OH^-(aq)$
2 $K_w = [H_3O^+(aq)][OH^-(aq)]$ or
   $K_w = [H^+(aq)][OH^-(aq)]$
3 $[H^+(aq)] = [OH^-(aq)] = 1.0 \times 10^{-7}\ mol\ dm^{-3}$
4 $K_w = 1.0 \times 10^{-14\ mol2}\ dm^{-6}$

Ionic radius
Order of radii: $Na > Mg > Na^+ > Mg^{2+}$
Order of radii: $O > F > O^{2-} > F^-$

But note that an oxygen atom is only very slightly bigger than an fluorine atom so it is very hard to see the difference in the size of the two smaller circles.

Increases: charge on the nucleus

Stays the same: electron configuration (all the ions have the same electron configuration as a neon atom).

Decreases: ionic radius

Ionisation enthalpy
a potassium
b silicon
c calcium
d aluminium

1 1
2 2
3 sodium

Shielding by inner full shells in the atoms of the elements in group 1 means that the 'effective nuclear charge' in each atom is 1+. Down the group, the outer electron is held less strongly being further from the same effective nuclear charge, so is more easily removed. Therefore, the first ionisation enthalpy for potassium is lower than that for sodium.

Iron extraction
a Charge of iron ore, coke and limestone
b Blast of hot air
c Molten slag
d Molten iron
e Tap hole

Coke burning in air heats the furnace.

$C(s) + O_2(g) \rightarrow CO_2(g)$

Coke also produces the reducing agent by reacting with carbon dioxide.

$C(s) + CO_2(g) \rightarrow 2CO(g)$

The carbon monoxide reduces the ore to iron.

$Fe_2O_3(s) + 3CO(g) \rightarrow 2Fe(l) + 3CO_2(g)$

Where the furnace is hot enough, carbon too can act as the reducing agent.

Limestone, $CaCO_3$, decomposes to calcium oxide, CaO, which combines with silicon dioxide and other impurities to make a liquid slag. For example:

$CaO(s) + SiO_2(s) \rightarrow CaSiO_3(l)$

Isomerism

Geometric: for example, *cis* and *trans* but-2-ene

Optical: for example, the mirror image forms of $CH_3CHOHCO_2H$

Chain: for example, butane and 2-methylpropane

Position: for example, propan-1-ol and propan-2-ol

Functional group: for example, propanoic acid and ethyl methanoate.

Isotopes

a	1	g	6
b	1	h	38
c	1	i	38
d	1	j	38
e	6	k	52
f	8	l	38

K_a

1    $HCO_2H(aq) + H_2O(l) \rightleftharpoons H_3O^+(aq) + HCO_2^-(aq)$

or

$HCO_2H(aq) \rightleftharpoons H^+(aq) + HCO_2^-(aq)$

2    $K_a = \dfrac{[H_3O^+(aq)][HCO_2^-(aq)]}{[HCO_2H(aq)]}$

or $K_a = \dfrac{[H^+(aq)][HCO_2^-(aq)]}{[HCO_2H(aq)]}$

3   In dilute solution the concentration of water is constant.

4   Phenol

5   Assumption 1: This assumption seems obvious from the equation for the ionisation of a weak acid, but it ignores the hydrogen ions from the ionisation of water. Water produces far fewer hydrogen ions than most weak acids, so its ionisation can be ignored.

Assumption 2: This assumes that only a very small proportion of the acid ionises. This is a riskier assumption which has to be checked because, in very dilute solutions, the degree of ionisation may become quite large relative to the amount of acid in the solution.

6   pH = 2.9

K_c

1   a $K_c = \dfrac{[HI(g)]^2}{[H_2(g)][I_2(g)]}$ no units

b $K_c = \dfrac{[PCl_3(g)][Cl_2(g)]}{[PCl_5(g)]}$ units: $mol\ dm^{-3}$

2    $K_c = 0.19\ mol\ dm^{-3}$

3   Amount of HI(g) = 10.22 mol

K_p

$K_p = \dfrac{(p_{HI})^2}{(p_{H_2})(p_{I_2})}$ no units

$K_p = \dfrac{(p_{NH_3})^2}{(p_{N_2})(p_{H_2})^3}$ Pa^{-2}

$K_p = \dfrac{(p_{NO_2})^2}{(p_{N_2O_4})}$ Pa

Ketones

a   No reaction

b   –

c   –

d   Reduction

e   Propan-2-ol

f $CH_3CHOHCH_3$

g CN^- ions in the presence of $H^+(aq)$ (from KCN and HCl(aq))

h   Addition (nucleophilic)

i $CH_3COH(CN)CH_3$

Le Chatelier's principle

1    $CH_2{=}CH_2(g) + H_2O(g) \rightleftharpoons CH_3CH_2OH(l)$

Higher pressure tends for force the equilibrium to the right (fewer moles of gas).

Lower temperature tends to favour the right-hand side, since the forward reaction is exothermic (but the temperature must be high enough for the reaction to proceed at a reasonable speed).

2    $CH_4(g) + H_2O(g) \rightleftharpoons CO(g) + 3H_2(g)$

Lower pressure favours the product side of the equilibrium since the forward reaction increases the number of moles of gas.

Raising the temperature favours the products because the forward reaction is endothermic. The limit is the cost of fuel for keeping the gas mixture hot.

3 **a** Adding water increases the degree of ionisation of the acid.

  b Increasing the concentration of ethanoate ions causes the equilibrium to shift to the left and reduces the extent of ionisation.

  c Increasing the concentration of oxonium ions also causes the equilibrium to shift to the left and reduces the extent of ionisation.

  d Hydroxide ions neutralise the oxonium ions. Adding an equivalent amount of alkali would convert almost all the acid to sodium ethanoate. The solution would be slightly alkaline because the ethanoate ion is a base.

$$CH_3CO_2^-(aq) + H_2O(l) \rightleftharpoons$$
$$CH_3CO_2H(aq) + OH^-(aq)$$

Lewis acids and bases

Lewis acids: H^+, Ni^{2+}, $AlCl_3$

Lewis bases: H_2O, NH_3, Cl_2

A Lewis acid is a molecule or ion that can form a bond by accepting a pair of electrons.

A Lewis base is a molecule or ion that can form a bond by donating a pair of electrons.

Ligands

Monodentate: H_2O, NH_3

Bidentate: ethanedioate ion, 1,2-diaminoethane

Hexadentate: EDTA ion

Markovnikov's rule

Missing words in order: alkene, hydrogen, most.

Products: 1-bromopropane, 2-methylpropan-1-ol

From left to right: primary < secondary < tertiary (< shows order of statbility)

Missing words in order: inductive, spreading, carbocations, electrophilic, secondary, stable.

Mass spectrometry (AS)

A	4	E	8
B	1	F	2
C	6	G	7
D	3	H	5

Average relative atomic mass

$$= \frac{(1.5 \times 2.04) + (23.6 \times 206) + (22.6 \times 207) + (52.3 \times 208)}{100}$$

$$= 207.2$$

Mass spectrometry (A2)

A 2
B 3
C 4
D 5
E 1

1 $C_2H_5OH + e^- \rightarrow C_2H_5OH^+ + 2e^-$

2 **a** $C_2H_5OH^+ \rightarrow CH_2OH^+ + CH_3\bullet$

  b The second fragment is an uncharged free radical, which is not accelerated or deflected in a mass spectrometer.

3 **a** This peak arises because some molecules of ethanol contain carbon-13 atoms. The isotope, carbon-13, makes up 1.1% of natural carbon.

  b This shows that ethanol contains two carbon atoms. In a molecule with two carbon atoms the $(M + 1)^+$ peak is 2.2% of the M^+ peak.

Maxwell–Boltzmann distribution

Vertical axis: number of molecules with kinetic energy, E
Horizontal axis: Kinetic energy, E

Curve with higher peak: distribution at lower temperature

More widely spread curve with lower peak: distribution at a higher temperature

Short vertical line to the right of the peaks: activation energy

Proportion of molecules able to react at a particular temperature: area to right of activation energy line between the curve and the x-axis

Molecules only react if they collide with enough energy between them to overcome the energy barrier: they must collide with energy equal to or greater than the activation energy. At around room temperature, only a small proportion of molecules have enough energy to react. At a higher temperature that proportion of molecules increases as the distribution of molecular energies shifts to the right.

Metallic bonding

a Metals can bend and stretch without breaking.
b Strong metallic bonding throughout the crystals.
c Delocalised electrons free to move in the metal crystals.
d Solvent molecules cannot bond with metal atoms strongly enough to break up the giant structure.

Molecular formula

a NH_3

b 17

c C_4H_{10}

d HO

e H_2O_2

Nitration of benzene

Conditions: a mixture of concentrated nitric and sulfuric acid.

$$HO^+{-}NO_2 \rightarrow H_2O + NO_2{}^+$$
$$\text{H}$$

Missing words: electrophilic substitution.

Aromatic nitro compounds are useful as explosives (for example, TNT).; they can also be reduced to amines used to make dyestuffs.

Nitric acid manufacture

$$4NH_3(g) + 5O_2 \rightleftharpoons 4NO(g) + 6H_2O(g)$$
$$2NO(g) + O_2(g) \rightleftharpoons 2NO_2(g)$$
$$4NO_2(g) + O_2(g) + 2H_2O(l) \rightarrow 4HNO_3(l)$$

Nitriles

a 1-iodopropane, $CH_3CH_2CH_2I$

b butanamide, $CH_3CH_2CH_2CONH_2$

c butanoic acid, $CH_3CH_2CH_2CO_2H$

d butylamine, $CH_3CH_2CH_2CH_2NH_2$

e $CH_3CH_2CH_2OH$

f $CH_3CH_2CH_2CN$,

g Heat under reflux with mineral acid, $H_3O^+(aq)$

This series of reactions converts an alcohol to an acid. The acid has one more carbon atom and so this series of reactions extends the carbon skeleton.

nmr spectroscopy

A 3

B 2

C 4

D 1

Nucleophilic addition

1 Cyanide ions, hydride ions

2 The C=O bond is polar. Because oxygen is highly electronegative, the C end of the bond is δ+.

3

4

Nucleophilic substitution

Top mechanism: S_N2. Rate = $k[C_4H_9Br][OH^-]$. The single step is the rate-determining step.

Bottom mechanism: S_N1. Rate = $k[C_4H_9Br]$. The first step is the rate-determining step.

Optical isomerism

1 Chiral

2 Enantiomers

3 Lactic

4 Stereoisomers

5 Asymmetry

6 Polarised

7 Active site

Revealed word: racemic

Orders of reaction

Concentration–time graphs: **A** – second (half-life doubles if initial concentration halves), **B** – zero (constant rate), **C** – first (constant half-life)

Rate–concentration graphs: **D** – first, **E** – second, **F** – zero

Organic preparations

Carrying out the reaction: **A**, **F**

Separating the product: **B**, **H**, **J**, **L**

Purifying the product: **B**, **C**, **D**, **H**, **O**

Identifying the product: **E**, **G**, **I**, **K**, **M**, **N**

Organic synthesis

A Heat under reflux with KCN in ethanol

B Heat under reflux with aqueous strong acid

C PCl_5 at room temperature

D $(CH_3)_2CHCH_2OH$ at room temperature

E Warm with a mixture of concentrated nitric and sulfuric acids

F Reduce by heating under reflux with tin and hydrochloric acid

G Treat with nitrous acid (HNO_2) below 10 °C

H Mix with a cold solution of phenol

I Heat under reflux with excess acidified potassium dichromate(VI)

J Reduce with $LiAlH_4$ in ether then add water

K Warm the mixture with a sulfuric acid catalyst

Oxidation numbers

1	-2	9	oxidised
2	$+5$	10	reduced
3	$+5$	11	oxidised
4	$+1$	12	reduced
5	$+5$	13	1, 5, 3, 3, 3, 3
6	$+2$	14	1, 4, 1, 2, 2
7	-1	15	1, 2, 1, 1, 1
8	$+4$	16	1, 8, 5, 1, 5, 4

Oxides

Basic: BaO, CaO, CuO, Cu_2O, MgO, Na_2O, PbO
Amphoteric: Al_2O_3, BeO, PbO_2, ZnO
Acidic: CO_2, NO_2, P_2O_3, P_2O_5, SO_2, SO_3
Neutral: CO, N_2O, NO

Oxidising agents

Oxygen, potassium dichromate(VI), bromine, potassium manganate(VII), chlorine, hydrogen peroxide.

Partial pressures

Missing words in order: sum, total pressure, reactions, p_B, p_C, $X_A p_{total}$, $X_C p_{total}$.

Period 3 chlorides

Sodium chloride: $NaCl$, solid, giant, ionic, none

Magnesium chloride: $MgCl_2$, solid, giant, ionic, slight

Aluminium chloride: $AlCl_3$, solid, giant, polarised ionic, considerable

Silicon chloride: $SiCl_4$, liquid, molecular, covalent in the molecules, complete

Phosphorus chlorides: PCl_3, liquid, molecular, covalent in the molecules, complete; PCl_5, solid, molecular vapour (but $PCl_4^+PCl_6^-$ in the solid state), covalent between P and Cl, complete.

$AlCl_3(aq) + 3H_2O(l) \rightarrow Al(OH)_3(s) + 3H^+(aq) + 3Cl^-(aq)$

$SiCl_4(aq) + 4H_2O(l) \rightarrow H_4SiO_4(s) + 4H^+(aq) + 4Cl^-(aq)$

$PCl_3(aq) + 3H_2O(l) \rightarrow H_3PO_3(s) + 3H^+(aq) + 3Cl^-(aq)$

Period 3 elements

Period 3 oxides

Magnesium oxide: MgO, solid, giant, ionic, basic

Silicon oxide: SiO_2, solid, giant, covalent, acidic

Sulfur oxide: SO_2, gas, molecular, covalent in the molecules, acidic

$MgO(s) + H_2O(l) \rightarrow Mg(OH)_2(s)$, alkaline suspension around pH = 9

$SO_2(g) + H_2O(l) \rightarrow H_2SO_3(s)$, acidic solution around pH = 1–2 depending on the concentration

Periodic table

1	Nitrogen	6	Period
2	Fluorine	7	Lithium
3	Alkaline earths	8	Alkali metals
4	Atomic number	9	Group
5	Noble gases	10	Halogens

Revealing the name: transition

Periodicity of physical properties

1   Giant structures: Li, Be, B, C, Na, Mg, Al, Si

2   Molecular: N, O, F, Ne, P, Si, Cl, Ar

3   Metallic: Li, Be, Na, Mg, Al

4   Covalent: B, C, N, O, F, Si, P, S, Cl

5   Transition from giant to molecular structures. Weak intermolecular forces mean that molecular solids are relatively easy to melt.

6   Charge on the nucleus increases thus increasing the attraction for the outer electrons which are all in the same main shell.

7   The 2s orbital is full at Be, there is then a slight dip as the next electron goes into a p orbital with a slightly higher energy.

8   The three p orbitals each have one electron in a nitrogen atom. The dip at oxygen happens as the next electron has to pair up with another electron. The repulsion between the two paired electrons results in a lower value of the energy required to remove an electron from a gaseous oxygen atom.

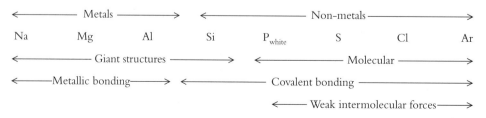

9 Ionisation energies decrease down a group. Down a group, the number of full shells increases. The increased shielding effect compensates for the increasing charge on the nucleus. The outer electrons get further and further away from the same effective nuclear charge, so they are easier to remove.

pH

$pH = -\log[H^+(aq)]$

or strictly $pH = -\log\left(\dfrac{[H^+(aq)]}{mol\ dm^{-3}}\right)$

$[H^+(aq)] = 10^{-pH}$

$K_w = [H^+(aq)][OH^-(aq)]$

$K_a = [H^+(aq)][A^-(aq)]/\ [HA(aq)]$

$pK_a = -\log K_a$

a = 2

b = 10

c = 2.9

d = 1

Date = 1909

pH changes during acid–base titrations

A Strong acid–weak base (methyl orange or methyl red)

B Weak acid–weak base (no suitable indicator)

C Strong acid–strong base (any of the indicators)

D Weak acid–strong base (phenolphthalein)

Phenol

1	Bakelite	5	Acidity
2	Thermosetting	6	Antiseptics
3	Delocalised	7	Electrophilic
4	Sodium		

Reagent: bromine.

pK_a

1 $pK_a = -\log K_a$

2 Phenol

3 Sulfurous acid

4 Hydrogensulfate ion

5 pH = 4.8

6 Ethanoic or methanoic acid

7 Phenol

8 A mixture of methanoic acid and sodium methanoate. Concentrations: [methanoate ion] = 1.6 × [methanoic acid]

Polar covalent bonds

Polar bonds (with the more electronegative, $\delta-$, atom on the right in each case): C—Br, C=O, C—O, H—O, I—Cl, H—S, S=O.

Polar molecules

All the bonds are polar except CH bonds.

Molecules are overall non-polar if the polarities cancel out.

CO_2 and $BeCl_2$ are linear.

H_2O and SO_2 are angular.

Note that CH_2Cl_2 and $SiCl_4$ are tetrahedral.

Molecules which are overall polar: CH_2Cl_2, H_2O, SO_2.

Proteins

a Primary

b Tertiary

c Secondary

d Quaternary

$$-\overset{|}{\underset{|}{C}}-\overset{\overset{O}{\|}}{C}-\overset{}{\underset{H}{N}}-\overset{|}{\underset{|}{C}}-$$

Rate constant

1 Rate = 6.9×10^{-8} mol dm^{-3} s^{-1}

2 Rate = $k[CH_3CO_2CH_3][OH^-]$

Rate = 5.6×10^{-5} mol dm^{-3} s^{-1}

Rate-determining step

a $2NH_3(aq) + OCl^-(aq) \rightarrow$
$N_2H_4(aq) + H_2O(l) + Cl^-(aq)$

b Step 2

c Rate = $k[NH_3]^2$

Rate equation

1 $CH_3CHO(g) \rightarrow CH_4(g) + CO(g)$
Rate = $k[CH_3CHO(g)]^2$,
units of k are mol^{-1} dm^3 s^{-1}

2 $\underset{CH_2}{CH_2 - CH_2(g)} \rightarrow CH_3CH = CH_2(g)$

Rate = $k\left[\underset{CH_2}{CH_2 - CH_2(g)}\right]$, units of k are s^{-1}

3 $2NO(g) + Br_2(g) \rightarrow 2NOBr(g)$
Rate = $k[NO(g)]^2[Br_2(g)]$,
units of k are mol^{-2} dm^6 s^{-1}

4 $2H_2(g) + 2NO(g) \rightarrow 2H_2O(g) + N_2(g)$
Rate = $k[H_2(g)][\ NO(g)]^2$,
units of k are mol^{-2} dm^6 s^{-1}

5 $2N_2O(g) \rightarrow 2N_2(g) + O_2(g)$
Rate = $k[N_2O(g)]$,
units of k are s^{-1}

Rates of reaction

1 B
2 D
3 A
4 C

Reaction mechanisms

1 $CH_3CH_2CH_2CH_2Br + NaOH \rightarrow$
$\quad\quad\quad CH_3CH_2CH_2CH_2OH + NaBr(aq)$
Nucleophilic substitution
Hydroxide ion, OH^-

2 $CH_2=CH_2 + Br_2 \rightarrow CH_2Br—CH_2Br$
Electrophilic addition
Bromine molecule, Br_2

3 $CH_3COCH_3 + HCN \rightarrow CH_3COH(CN)CH_3$
Nucleophilic addition
Cyanide ion, CN^-

4 $CH_3CH_3 + Cl_2 \rightarrow CH_3—CH_2Cl + HCl$
Free-radical substitution (chain reaction)
Chlorine atoms, Cl•

5 $C_6H_6 + NO_2^+ \rightarrow C_6H_5NO_2 + H^+$
Electrophilic substitution
Nitryl cation, NO_2^+

Recrystallisation

Step **E**: Solid dissolved in the minimum amount of
solvent needed.

Step **B**: Cooled to crystallise the product leaving
impurities in solution.

Step **A**: Filtered to separate the purified crystals from
the solvent with impurities, then rinsed with
the minimum volume of cold solvent needed
to wash away traces of impurities in the
solvent.

Step **D**: Solvent allowed to evaporate from the filtered
crystals.

Step **C**: To measure the melting point as a test for
purity.

Recycling

1 Recycling steel: N, D, H, K, B or N, B, D, H, K
2 Recycling aluminium: C, L, A, J, F
3 Recycling plastics: M, O, E, I, G

Redox reactions

Oxidising agents: chlorine, bromine, hydrogen peroxide,
iodine, nitric acid, oxygen, potassium dichromate(VI),
potassium manganate(VI)

Reducing agents: hydrogen, sulfur dioxide, zinc with
acid.

$$2Fe^{3+}(aq) + 2I^-(aq) \rightarrow I_2(aq) + 2Fe^{2+}(aq)$$

$$I_2(aq) + 2S_2O_3^{2-}(aq) \rightarrow 2I^-(aq) + S_4O_6^{2-}(aq)$$

$$2MnO_4^-(aq) + 6H^+(aq) + 5H_2O_2(aq) \rightarrow$$
$$2Mn^{2+}(aq) + 5O_2(g) + 8H_2O(l)$$

$$Br_2(aq) + SO_2(aq) + 2H_2O(l) \rightarrow$$
$$2Br^-(aq) + SO_4^{2-}(s) + 4H^+(aq)$$

Redox titrations

Missing numbers in order: 294, 294, 0.250, 294, 0.250,
0.020, 6, 14, 3, 2, 3, 6, 6, 0.025, 0.020, 0.030, 6, 0.025,
0.020, 6, 0.025, 0.020, 0.030.

Concentration = 0.10 mol dm^{-3}

Reversible reactions

a Raise the pressure or lower the temperature
b Lower the pressure or raise the temperature
c Add alkali to lower the hydrogen ion concentration
d Add acid to raise the hydrogen ion concentration

But note that there are possible alternative correct
answers.

Shapes of molecules

Skeletal formulae

A C_8H_{18}; $CH_3CH(CH_3)CH(CH_3)CH_2CH_2CH_3$;
2,3-dimethylhexane

B C_6H_{10}

Cyclohexene

C $C_3H_6O_2$; $CH_3CH_2CO_2H$; propanoic acid

D C_5H_{10}; $CH_3CH_2CH=CHCH_3$; *cis*-pent-2-ene

E $C_6H_{14}O$; $(CH_3)_2COHCH_2CH_2CH_3$;
2-methylpentan-2-ol

F $C_6H_{12}O_2$; $CH_3CH_2CH_2CO$—OCH_2CH_3;
ethyl butanoate

Stability

Reactants energetically stable relative to products.

Reactants energetically unstable relative to products but kinetically stable (inert).

Reactants energetically stable relative to products.

Reactants energetically and kinetically unstable relative to products.

Structural isomerism

Chain isomerism: butane, 2-methylpropane

Position isomerism: propan-1-ol and propan-2-ol

Functional group isomerism: propanal and propanone

Sulfuric acid manufacture

$C \rightarrow D \rightarrow B \rightarrow A \rightarrow E$

$S(l) + O_2(g) \rightarrow SO_2(g)$

$2SO_2(g) + O_2(g) \rightleftharpoons 2SO_3(g)$

$H_2O(l) + SO_3(g) \rightarrow H_2SO_4(l)$

Catalyst: V_2O_5

Rate of reaction: raising the temperature, using the V_2O_5 catalyst and in some plants increasing the pressure.

Conversion: three factors contribute to converting as much of sulfur dioxide as possible to sulfur trioxide: cooling the gas mixture after passing through each catalyst bed, adding more of one of the reactants (oxygen) and removing the product (sulfur dioxide).

Tests for organic functional groups

1	F	5	D
2	E	6	A
3	C	7	G
4	H	8	B

Transition metals

1	Copper	7	Iron
2	Nickel	8	Manganese
3	Vanadium	9	Chromium
4	Copper	10	Vanadium
5	Iron	11	Iron
6	Copper	12	Nickel

Ultraviolet and visible spectroscopy

1	UV	4	UV
2	Visible	5	Visible
3	UV	6	Visible

A Ni^{2+}
B $Cr_2O_7^{2-}$
C Cu^{2+}
D Co^{2+}

Yield calculations

Reasons why the overall yield may be low:

- the reaction may be incomplete (perhaps because it is slow or because it reaches an equilibrium state), so that a proportion of the starting chemicals fails to react,
- there may be side reactions producing by-products instead of the required chemical,
- recovery of all the product from the reaction mixture is usually impossible,
- some of the product is usually lost during transfer of the chemicals from one container to another as the product is separated and purified.

4 Theoretical yield = 26.7 g
Percentage yield = 88%

5 Theoretical yield = 51 g
Percentage yield = 29%

Multiple choice tests

Question number	Physical	Inorganic	Organic
1	A	C	C
2	D	C	B
3	D	D	B
4	C	D	D
5	C	A	A
6	C	A	C
7	B	B	A
8	C	D	C
9	B	C	A
10	A	D	D
11	C	B	D
12	A	C	B
13	A	C	B
14	B	A	B
15	A	A	A
16	B	B	D
17	A	B	A
18	C	A	A
19	B	C	B
20	D	B	D
21	A	D	C
22	D	A	C
23	D	A	A
24	B	D	D
25	D	D	B
26	C	D	C
27	A	A	B
28	D	B	C
29	B	C	A
30	C	B	C

Order form

A-Z

Tick the relevant box if you wish to order a title on approval or inspection. Only fill in the quantity and value columns if you are making a firm order.

Inspection Copies – *Educational establishments only*. If your recommendation will result in the purchase of 15 or more copies in a year, the inspection copy may be retained free of charge.

Approval Copies – the book(s) must be paid for in full or returned in mint condition within 30 days from date of invoice.

> **For details of current special offers, call Millie Patel on: (020) 7873 6372.**

Please send me the following:

Title	ISBN		Price	Inspection (✓)	Approval (✓)	Firm order Quantity	Value £
Key Stage 3 A-Z Handbooks							
Key Stage 3 A-Z English Handbook	0 340 80016 X	June	approx £4.99	☐	◼	....	....
Key Stage 3 A-Z Maths Handbook	0 340 80017 8	June	approx £4.99	☐	◼	....	....
Key Stage 3 A-Z Science Handbook	0 340 80018 6	June	approx £4.99	☐	◼	....	....
GCSE A-Z Handbooks							
GCSE A-Z Biology Handbook	0 340 75357 9		£7.99	☐	◼	....	....
GCSE A-Z Business Studies Handbook	0 340 68366 X		£7.99	☐	◼	....	....
GCSE A-Z Double Award Science Handbook	0 340 73060 9		£7.99	☐	◼	....	....
GCSE A-Z Geography Handbook	0 340 72447 1		£7.99	☐	◼	....	....
A-Z Coursework Handbooks							
A-Z Business Studies Coursework Handbook, Second Edition	0 340 80289 8	June	approx £6.99	☐	◼	....	....
A-Z Geography Coursework Handbook, Second Edition	0 340 80290 1	June	approx £6.99	☐	◼	....	....
A-Z Psychology Coursework Handbook	0 340 79063 6	Sept	approx £6.99	☐	◼	....	....
A-Z Sociology Coursework Handbook, Second Edition	0 340 80291 X	June	approx £6.99	☐	◼	....	....
A-Z Workbooks							
A-Z Business Studies Workbook	0 340 79981 1	January	approx £6.99	☐	◼	....	....
A-Z Chemistry Workbook	0 340 79982 X	August	approx £6.99	☐	◼	....	....
A-Z Sociology Workbook	0 340 79983 8	August	approx £6.99	☑	◼	....	....

Title	ISBN	Price	Inspection (✓)	Approval (✓)	Firm order Quantity	Value £

The Complete A-Z Handbooks

Title	ISBN	Price	Inspection (✓)	Approval (✓)	Quantity	Value £
The Complete A-Z Accounting Handbook	0 340 69124 7	£9.99	☐	■	....	....
The Complete A-Z Biology Handbook, Second Edition	0 340 77221 2	£9.99	☐	■	....	....
The Complete A-Z Business Studies CD-ROM	0 340 68847 5	£60.99 + VAT	■	☐	....	....
The Complete A-Z Business Studies Handbook, Third Edition	0 340 77214 X	£9.99	☐	■	....	....
The Complete A-Z Chemistry Handbook, Second Edition	0 340 77218 2	£9.99	☐	■	....	....
The Complete A-Z Economics & Business Studies Handbook, Second Edition	0 340 77216 6	£9.99	☐	■	....	....
The Complete A-Z Economics Handbook	0 340 78954 9 August	approx £9.99	☐	■	....	....
The Complete A-Z English Literature Handbook	0 340 78291 9 August	approx £9.99	☐	■	....	....
The Complete A-Z Geography Handbook, Second Edition	0 340 77217 4	£9.99	☐	■	....	....
The Complete A-Z Health and Social Care Handbook	0 340 70557 4	£9.99	☐	■	....	....
The Complete A-Z ICT and Computing Handbook	0 340 80277 4 October	approx £9.99	☐	■	....	....
The Complete A-Z Law Handbook	0 340 72120 0	£9.99	☐	■	....	....
The Complete A-Z Leisure, Travel and Tourism Handbook	0 340 64789 2	£9.99	☐	■	....	....
The Complete A-Z Mathematics Handbook, Second Edition	0 340 78030 4	£9.99	☐	■	....	....
The Complete A-Z Media and Communication Handbook	0 340 69131 X	£9.99	☐	■	....	....
The Complete A-Z Physical Education Handbook	0 340 77213 1	£9.99	☐	■	....	....
The Complete A-Z Physics Handbook, Second Edition	0 340 77219 0	£9.99	☐	■	....	....
The Complete A-Z Psychology Handbook, Second Edition	0 340 77215 8	£9.99	☐	■	....	....
The Complete A-Z Sociology Handbook, Second Edition	0 340 77220 4	£9.99	☐	■	....	....
The Complete A-Z 19th and 20th Century British History Handbook	0 340 67378 8	£9.99	☐	■	....	....
The Complete A-Z 20th Century European History Handbook	0 340 67996 4	£10.99	☐	■	....	....

TOTAL VALUE OF ORDER £ [_____]

METHODS OF PAYMENT

Fill in your name and address and we will send the books to you with an invoice. If you would prefer to send payment with your order, you can pay by cheque or, for immediate service, please telephone our credit card hotline.

Payment by cheque
☐ I enclose a cheque/postal order for £_____
   Please make cheques payable to Bookpoint Ltd.

UK Schools/Colleges only
☐ Please send to my school/college with invoice
   I attach my Requisition No _____

Payment by credit card
Credit card telephone hotline – 01235 822770.

Please return this form to: Bookpoint Ltd, Hodder & Stoughton Educational, Direct Services, FREEPOST OF 1488, Abingdon, Oxon, OX14 4YY

Prices may be changed without notice.
Requests for titles not yet published will be recorded and sent immediately on publication.

Please remember to fill in your name and address

Surname

Initials   Mr Mrs Miss Ms Other

Job Title

Department

School/College

Address

County

Postcode   Telephone number

Orders may be phoned or faxed to our Direct Services department on tel: 01235 827720 fax: 01235 400454 e-mail: orders@bookpoint.co.uk

www.hodderheadline.co.uk